This important new ... a vital correction to ... biblical teaching on ... judgment. It also gives a clear biblical presentation of the destiny of the believers in the age to come. This excellent book strengthens our hope in eternity as it deals with some very important scripture texts. I strongly recommend it.

—MIKE BICKLE
INTERNATIONAL HOUSE OF PRAYER OF KANSAS CITY

Here is a book on a topic that is sorely needed in our day. So it is with joy I commend this work to you, even though I may still have some differences on some smaller points of exegesis. The central message of this work, however, is desperately needed; for all too many have handled (or even failed to handle) many of these texts in such a careless way that reverses the straightforward meaning of these scriptures. Thank you, Daniel, for calling our attention once again back to the Word of God.

—WALTER C. KAISER JR.
PRESIDENT EMERITUS
GORDON-CONWELL THEOLOGICAL SEMINARY

What happens to us after we die? It's a question that's often on the minds of people, but not so often talked about. In this concise volume, Dan Juster has captured the range of biblical teaching on heaven, hell, and the afterlife without reducing that teaching into narrow dogma. Dan provides an accessible resource for understanding and discussing these issues that is always engaging and sometimes surprising as well.

—Russ Reznik
Former Executive Director of the Union of
Messianic Jewish Congregations

Open the pages of this book and get ready to embark on a journey through the Word of God detailing a subject that has been the debate of theologians, mystics, teachers, and believers in every religion since the dawn of time: the afterlife. Is there a heaven? A hell? What happens to us when we are no longer living on this earth? Dan's exhaustive scriptural study of this important subject, interspersed with accounts of near-death experiences, will provide the reader with sufficient material with which to draw his or her own conclusions. A valuable resource for those whose hearts are searching for biblical answers concerning the afterlife.

—Jane Hansen Hoyt
President/CEO, Aglow International

God is this loving old Father who will always care and never ask for anything. Is He really only an old loving Father, or is God more? Dan Juster, my dear friend, is pursuing this question in the Scriptures and arrives with an interesting conclusion. There is really heaven and hell and a God who is a loving judge of all.

—Martin Buehlmann
Leader of the Vineyard Movement
Germany, Austria, Switzerland

Daniel Juster takes issue with the dangers of modernism by taking the reader through the entire Bible regarding the reality of divine judgment and its eternal consequences. He carefully acknowledges places where the meaning of the text is unclear but also carefully draws our attention to the clear teaching of the Word of God. Reading this book will lead one to repent and believe in the gospel!

—Dr. Doug Beacham
General Superintendent, International
Pentecostal Holiness Church

Dan Juster is one of the most levelheaded, open-minded, widely read theologians I know, willing to follow the truth wherever it leads. In a day when so many are abandoning fundamental biblical truths, Dan is a first-rate guide.

—Michael L. Brown, PhD
President, FIRE School of Ministry

A clear, concise, and balanced survey of what the Scriptures teach about final destinies. Juster's work is a timely wake-up call for the body of Messiah and the postmodern world in which we live. I highly recommend it to all who want to avoid thinking about this subject.

—David Rudolph, PhD, Cambridge
Director of Messianic Jewish Studies
The King's University, Dallas, Texas

I find that when I read a book and really like it this is often because I already believe most if not all that the author is teaching but have never put that teaching into an orderly teaching that the book helps to articulate truth. This is what I find in Dan Juster's book—a very meticulous, thorough, clear presentation of truth regarding the afterlife.

—Don Finto
Pastor Emeritus, Belmont Church, Nashville, Tennessee
Church Father, City of Nashville
Caleb Company

HEAVEN
HELL
and the
AFTERLIFE

DANIEL JUSTER, THD

**CREATION
HOUSE**

HEAVEN, HELL, AND THE AFTERLIFE: WHAT THE BIBLE
REALLY SAYS
by Daniel C. Juster
Published by Creation House
A Charisma Media Company
600 Rinehart Road
Lake Mary, Florida 32746
www.charismamedia.com

Unless otherwise noted, all Scripture quotations are from
the Holy Bible, New International Version. Copyright © 1973,
1978, 1984, 2010, 2011, International Bible Society. Used by
permission.

Scripture quotations marked KJV are from the King James
Version of the Bible.

Scripture quotations marked NKJV are from the New King
James Version of the Bible. Copyright © 1979, 1980, 1982 by
Thomas Nelson, Inc., publishers. Used by permission.

Cover design by Judith McKittrick Wright

Visit the author's website: www.tikkunministries.org.

Library of Congress Control Number: 2016963690
International Standard Book Number: 978-1-62999-195-5
E-book International Standard Book Number:
978-1-62999-196-2

While the author has made every effort to provide accurate telephone numbers and Internet addresses at the time of publication, neither the publisher nor the author assumes any responsibility for errors or for changes that occur after publication.

17 18 19 20 21— 9 8 7 6 5 4 3 2
Printed in the United States of America

CONTENTS

INTRODUCTION

THE QUESTION OF the final destiny of individuals after death is one of the most important questions that can be asked. Is there life after death? What is it like? Is there a heaven and a hell? Is our destiny as human beings either heaven or hell? Or, is there another destiny taught in the Bible? How does one make sure that they will attain a good and happy final destiny after death? How inclusive is the hope for a good final destiny? What is heaven like? Is there an age to come on earth? What is it like? What is hell like?

Throughout history theologians have answered these questions but with very different answers. This is because the Bible gives many different slants on every one of these questions. These slants or pictures can be harmonized, but there are different ways of harmonizing. Which verses are primary, clear, and didactic; and which are of limited value in answering the questions?

I believe a survey of the Bible is the right way forward. This survey needs to look at every significant text in context. We need to weigh the question of just what the biblical writer under the inspiration of the Holy Spirit is claiming to teach in every text.

Today the evangelical world is responding to new teachers who claim to be evangelicals whose views are close to universalism. This is the teaching that almost every human being will attain a positive postmortal final destiny. We have this view in the "almost universalism" of Rob Bell (*Love Wins*)[1] to the scholarly writing of Douglas Campbell of Duke Divinity School in *The Deliverance of God*.[2] The famous evangelical Anglican John Stott, in his last years, presented annihilation as the final destiny of the lost. Eternal suffering in hell, in his view, could not be squared with an ultimately redeemed universe and a God of love. Nor could he find evidence that all would be saved.[3] Then there are purgatorial ideas of hell that it is temporary, terrible, and of varying durations depending on the level of sin committed and needed purification.

The classical church confessions that included the confession of an afterlife were much clearer than the profession of many followers of Jesus today. There is much confusion. Judaism taught that all Jews would be saved except those whose sin was such as to repudiate the covenant. In addition, people from all nations could attain a positive life in the age to come if they abandoned idolatry and followed the basic laws of morality explained in terms of the Noachide Laws (the moral laws that were given to Noah for all humanity). This may sound quite tolerant unless we realize that this excludes most human beings that have ever lived. Pre-Vatican II Catholics taught that there was no salvation outside of the Catholic Church. Orthodox Christian teaching was very similar. One had to affirm the classic creeds as the foundational teaching of the Church. Evangelicals from the Reformation on basically taught that one had to be born again, and have an explicit personal faith relationship with Jesus, to attain a final good end. Some required baptism in water for this and some did not. Some required a definite born-again experience, but others accepted that one could be raised from childhood to be always believing. These were more in the infant baptism streams of Protestantism, whether or not it was necessary for them to enter heaven.

There are numerous books where authors were given visions of the age to come, heaven, hell, and others who even claimed to actually visit. It is not wise to build doctrine on these visions. Some confirm biblical teaching and some do not. They are not consistent with one another. However, to give some sense of this literature, I have concluded chapters with such accounts and short introductory comments. This will provide an interesting aside that will bring another aspect to our primarily didactic presentation.

So let's begin our survey of the Bible and evaluate the evidence.

PART I

THE HEBREW SCRIPTURES
AND THE AFTERLIFE

Chapter 1

THE AFTERLIFE IN THE TORAH

GOD CREATED HUMAN beings, male and female, in His image. The first parents of the human race therefore had a human dignity that superseded all of the other sentient creatures. Being in the image of God was defined in terms of rule. Human beings have all the capacities like God's that are needed for them to rule wisely in submitted partnership with the Father.

> So God created mankind in his own image, in the image of God he created them; male and female he created them. God blessed them and said to them, "Be fruitful and increase in number; fill the earth and subdue it. Rule over the fish in the sea and the birds in the sky and over every living creature that moves on the ground."
>
> —GENESIS 1:27–28

When God placed Adam and Eve in the Garden of Eden to work it and take care of it, He commanded them that they "must not eat from the tree of the knowledge of good and evil, for when you eat from it you will certainly die" (Gen. 2:17).

In chapter 3 we read that there was also a tree of life.

> He must not be allowed to reach out his hand and
> take also from the tree of life and eat, and live
> forever . . . So the Lord God . . . placed on the east
> side of the Garden of Eden cherubim and a flaming
> sword flashing back and forth to guard the way to
> the tree of life.
>
> —GENESIS 3:22–24

This combination of texts shows that human beings had such value that they were given a potential to live forever. Perhaps the way to the tree of life and eating its fruit was only an open opportunity had our first ancestors obeyed. The tree of life concept shows us that human beings at least had a possibility for everlasting life. Is this possibility now forever forfeited or can it be restored?

The promise of the seed to come from the woman who would crush the head of the serpent (Gen. 3:15) is a text of hope for restoration. The idea of a seed that will restore humanity continues throughout the biblical narrative and comes to fruition in Israel and then in the Messiah. The seed promise is passed to Noah and to his son Shem through Terah, Abraham's father, and then to Abraham. Through Abraham we read that "all peoples on earth will be blessed" (12:3). Does this blessing include the restoration of everlasting life? We are not explicitly told, but Genesis may be implying that hope. Most scholars today see Genesis 1–3 as eschatological and think that the Creation accounts and Garden of Eden foreshadow the eschatological or last days' fulfillment of the age to come. If so, that means that the tree of life opportunity can be offered to human beings again.

In Genesis 5:21–24 we find an intriguing and short passage about the pre-flood patriarch Enoch. We read:

> After he became the father of Methuselah, Enoch
> walked faithfully with God 300 years and had other
> sons and daughters. Altogether, Enoch lived a total
> of 365 years. Enoch walked faithfully with God;
> then he was no more, because God took him away.

At least in this case, we have an example of a man who apparently did not die but was taken by God to a different realm. The text does not say he died as it notes for the other patriarchs. So a change to live in another realm with God is at least a possibility for human beings!

As a side note here I call your attention to 2 Kings 2. It gives us the second and only example in the Bible of a person being translated and not undergoing death. The passage begins with the words: "When the LORD was about to take Elijah up to heaven in a whirlwind, Elijah and Elisha were on their way from Gilgal." The account of this translation is much more extensive than the translation of Enoch in Genesis 5:21ff. We read in 2 Kings, chapter 2, verses 11 and 12:

> As they were walking along and talking together,
> suddenly a chariot of fire and horses of fire appeared
> and separated the two of them, and Elijah went
> up to heaven in a whirlwind. Elisha saw this and
> cried out, "My father! My father! The chariots and
> horsemen of Israel!" And Elisha saw him no more.
> Then he took hold of his garment and tore it in two.

The vision of a chariot for the throne of God is found repeatedly in the Book of Ezekiel, but here it seems to be a divinely commissioned supernatural vehicle that takes Elijah to heaven or the abode of God. He is taken bodily! This is part of those passages of mysterious revelations such as the armies of God from heaven, angelic chariots and horses, and more. The prophet sees such things, but we cannot know how far to press the literal description.

In conclusion we have another passage which shows that not only can a person not die, but he can be bodily transformed and taken into heaven or the abode of God, a picture of the possibilities of the afterlife.

In Genesis 23 we read about the burial (entombment) of the body of Sarah. There is an extensive presentation of the purchase of the cave for the entombment. There is no explicit statement about the afterlife, but burial rites were important throughout the ancient world and no less so in the Middle East. Religious rituals emphasized assuring the dead a passage to a good afterlife. It is hard to believe that only Abraham and his descendants, the nation of Israel, would not have such beliefs about the afterlife. However, we shall see that this is not a primary emphasis in early sections of the Hebrew Bible.

In Genesis 25:8 we read that after Abraham died, an old man and full of years, he was "gathered to his people." His body was then placed in the same cave as Sarah's. Some Bible scholars believe that this phrase means more than just to have one's bones next to the bones of other family members. Rather, they think it implies that the person in some sense is rejoined to family members. His people are more than just Sarah whose body was in that same tomb. His people included others that died and were not in the proximity.

In Genesis 35:28–29 we read the same phrase as above. We do not read this phrase for the wives of the patriarchs that died. "Isaac lived a hundred and eighty years. Then he breathed his last and died and was gathered to his people."

In Genesis 42:38 Jacob protests the requirement to

bring his son Benjamin to Egypt and states that if harm comes to him, "You will bring my gray head down to the grave in sorrow." The word for *grave* here is *Sheol*. The word can just mean the grave or it can mean the abode of the dead in the underworld, which is sometimes described as a shadowy, unattractive existence of ghostlike figures. The text does not clarify, but the NIV simply interprets it as grave.

We read of the death of Jacob in Genesis 49:33: "When Jacob had finished giving instructions to his sons, he drew up his feet into the bed, breathed his last and was gathered to his people."

The passage about Joseph's death omits this phrase, but his body was embalmed after the traditions of Egypt (50:26). Before his death he made his brothers swear to carry his bones up from Egypt (v. 25). His body was placed in a coffin. This instruction was for the descendants.

The passage on the death of Aaron uses the same language as we found with the Patriarchs: "The LORD said to Moses and Aaron, 'Aaron will be gathered to his people. He will not enter the land I gave the Israelites'" (Num. 24:23–24, NKJV). After Aaron died, the nation mourned for him for thirty days (v. 29).

Finally, we read about the accounts of the death of Moses. The Lord tells him:

> Go up into the Abarim Range to Mount Nebo in Moab, across from Jericho, and view Canaan, the land I am giving the Israelites as their own possession. There on the mountain that you have climbed you will die and be gathered to your people,

just as your brother Aaron died on Mount Hor and
was gathered to his people.

—Deuteronomy 32:49–50

In Deuteronomy 34:5–6 we read:

And Moses the servant of the Lord died there in
Moab, as the Lord had said. He buried him in
Moab, in the valley opposite Beth Peor, but to this
day no one knows where his grave is.

The Israelites grieved for Moses for thirty days (v. 8).
This is a very interesting passage since "gathered to his
people" cannot mean that his dead body was put in a
grave with other ancestors. His body was buried by God
in a place alone, and no one knew or knows where it is.
Furthermore, the body was not gathered to the mourners
for grieving and burial. It looks like being gathered is to
be rejoined to relatives.

We do not have much information in the Torah on the
afterlife. We have the hope with regard to the tree of life,
the seed promise, and the blessing to come from Abraham
to the nations. There is a hint that life goes on after death
in the phrase, "to be gathered to his people."

DANTE

Dante Alighieri wrote the most famous presentation of
hell in Western history. It was written in the fourteenth
century. It is written as a fictional imaginary depiction, but
who knows the influences of the mind. Many levels of hell
were described with lesser and weightier sufferings. It has
been a most influential picture. The present version is a
modern translation from 2011. The following is a selection
from lower levels:

Canto V

I came into a place that was completely dark,
Bellowing as the sea does in a storm,
When opposing winds clash on each side.

This hurricane that never rests
Hurtles the spirits onward in its forceful gale;
Whirling them round, beating and smashing them.
When they arrive at the edge of the precipice,
Then come the shrieks, the cries, and the sorrowful
    wails,
There they blaspheme God and all his power:

I learned that this was the place of punishment
For those who were condemned for their lust,
Who followed their personal passions instead of
    reason.

And as the wings of birds drive them forward
In huge flocks in the winter months,
So does that blast always propel these evil spirits;

Left, right, downward, upward, it drives them:
They have no hope of comfort forever,
Nor of rest, or sleep, or even of lesser pain.

Canto VII

Here I saw more people than anywhere else,
Some on one side and some on the other, grunting
    and howling.
Rolling huge stone boulders forward by brute force
    along.

They clashed together, and then at the point of
    impact
Each one turned around, rolling their stone the
    other way,
Crying, "Why do you hoard?"
And, "Why do you squander?"

Thus they returned along the gloomy circle
One group on each side, to the opposite point,
Shouting their shameful cries the entire time.

Then each when he reached the other end, wheeled
    about
Through his half-circle to begin another joust:
And I, with great pain in my heart,

Exclaimed: "My Master, now tell me
Who these people are, and if they were clergy,
These with shaven heads."
And he said to me;

"All of them were lacking intellect in the first Life.
Those on the right squandered everything
They had without restraint…

They are the clergy, with those who have no head
    covering
Their heads, and Popes and Cardinals, who
    hoarded
Everything, sometimes spending nothing at all.

It is their hoarding and squandering that has
Put them in this state,
And placed them in this scuffle.
They did it themselves and I will speak no more of
    it."

Canto XII

We with our faithful escort, move on
Along the brink of the boiling red river,
Where those who were boiling uttered loud
    laments.

I saw some people buried up to their eyebrows,
And the great Centaur said:
These are Tyrants,
Who dealt in bloodshed and in pillaging.

Here they lament their pitiless deeds;
He is Alexander, and fierce Dionysius,
Who brought Sicily many sorrowful years.[1]

Chapter 2

THE HISTORICAL/PROPHETIC BOOKS

F IRST SAMUEL 28:7–19 presents us with an important passage with implications on the afterlife. In this passage Saul visits a medium in Endor. Saul had previously expelled mediums and spiritists from the land of Israel. So when Saul in disguise went to visit this woman, she resisted helping him since such practices were illegal. She thought it was a trap and could bring her death. He asked the woman to bring up Samuel. "When the woman saw Samuel, she cried out at the top of her voice and said to Saul, 'Why have you deceived me? You are Saul'" (v. 12).

Clearly Saul believed that the soul or spirit of the dead continued to live on. In addition, in seeing Samuel the woman was given some kind of information to know that it was Saul who made the request. Saul asked her what she saw. The woman responded to Saul's question and said, "An old man wearing a robe is coming up" (v. 14).

Saul knew it was Samuel. We read, "Samuel said to Saul, 'Why have you disturbed me by bringing me up?'" (v. 15). So Saul explained his dire situation in his war with the Philistines and God's absence. We then read that Samuel gave Saul a clear rebuke for his past disobedience and stated that God would hand him and Israel over to the Philistines. Then he told Saul that he and his sons would be with him.

This passage raises many questions.

First of all, did the medium really have the ability to call up Samuel? Many Christian deliverance ministers believe that mediums call up demons that pretend to be the person and have sufficient non-natural knowledge to fool the participants. Yet here the woman herself thinks it is Samuel. On the other hand, she seems shocked that it is really Samuel. I think the best interpretation is that Samuel really was called by God to override the normal medium process and actually reveal himself to the medium and Saul. This would explain her screaming out and also her fear in the revelation that the person she was serving was Saul.

The prophetic word that Samuel gives to Saul is accurate and also confirms that this was really Samuel. So the passage does confirm some kind of life after death. Samuel's prophetic word states, "Tomorrow you and your sons will be with me. The Lord will also give the army of Israel into the hands of the Philistines" (v. 19).

Is Samuel saying that Saul and his sons will be in the same place with him? It appears to be so. Or does he only mean that they will be in the abode of the dead, but not exactly the same place? Samuel makes no distinction of location for Saul, his righteous son Jonathan, or himself.

It is best to not put too much weight on this passage with regard to the state of those who have died. There will be many other passages to integrate.

THE DEATH OF DAVID'S SON WITH BATHSHEBA

After Nathan rebuked David for his adultery with Bathsheba and for arranging the murder of her husband,

Uriah, we read the story of the death of his son as a result of God's judgment for this affair. We read the following words of David:

> While the child was still alive, I fasted and wept. I thought, "Who knows? The Lord may be gracious to me and let the child live." But now that he is dead, why should I go on fasting? Can I bring him back again? I will go to him, but he will not return to me.
> —2 SAMUEL 12:22–23

The text is an indication that ancient Israelites did not believe that the death of a person was their complete annihilation. Of course, one could see the text as merely metaphorical. He would have the same fate as his child; that is his body would be buried and he as a person would cease to be. However, in the light of common beliefs in the culture of the ancient Near East (today the Middle East), it is more likely to see a belief in some kind of soul continuation after death. The nature of that continuation is not clear.

RESURRECTIONS FROM THE DEAD IN ELIJAH AND ELISHA

Two resurrections from the dead are recorded in 1 Kings, one in the ministry of Elijah (1 Kings 17:17–24) and the other in the ministry of Elisha (2 Kings 4:15–37). In both of these cases a child was raised from the dead. The former child was the son of a woman who was given a miracle of provision by Elijah. The second was a child conceived after a prophetic word from Elisha. The accounts are similar. In both accounts the life of the child returns. These accounts could be a taken as hints of the possibility of a future resurrection or just as unusual miracles without implications. However, does something continue to exist, a soul/spirit that returns to the body, which is the nature of the language in the text?

The Language "Rested with His Fathers"

We noted previously in the patriarchal accounts where one was said to be "gathered to his people" at the time of death. In the books of Kings, the language used is "rested with his fathers." The phrase is not explained. It does not indicate that the person ceased to be; but could it be in some sense be a positive meaning in that there is no more strife and battle? It may imply more than just the rest of the body in a family tomb area. We read this phrase of David in 1 Kings 2:10, Solomon in 1 Kings 11:43, Jeroboam in 1 Kings 14:20, Rehoboam in 1 Kings 14:31, Abijam in 1 Kings 15:8, Asa in 1 Kings 15:24, Omri in 1 Kings 16:28, Ahab in 1 Kings 22:40, Jehoshaphat in 1 Kings 22:50, Jehu in 2 Kings 10:35, Jehoahaz in 2 Kings 13:9, Jehoash in 2 Kings 14:16, Jeroboam II in 2 Kings 14:29, Azariah in 2 Kings 15:7, Menahem in 2 Kings 15:22, Jotham in 2 Kings 15:38, Ahaz in 2 Kings 16:20, Hezekiah in 2 Kings 20:21, Manasseh in 2 Kings 21:18, and finally Jehoiakim in 2 Kings 24:6. There seems to be no differentiation between good and evil kings in this description. Its absence seems to be the case with those who did not have a normal burial. One could therefore wonder if the phrase supports soul sleep; the idea that the soul is still alive but in a state of unawareness until the judgment day. The texts are too limited in meaning to draw any firm conclusions.

A RESURRECTION FROM THE DEAD THROUGH TOUCHING THE BONES OF ELISHA

Elijah was taken up into heaven, but Elisha suffered from an illness from which he died (2 Kings 13:14). Once when some Israelites were burying a man, they fled from a band of Moabite raiders. They threw the body into the tomb of Elisha, probably a cave tomb; and when the body touched Elisha's bones, the man came to life and stood up (13:20–21). This text again shows that there is something beyond the physical, and that the soul/spirit can return to a body and it can be resurrected.

Though 1 and 2 Kings was completed after the Babylonian exile, 1 and 2 Chronicles was written much later. The phrase "rested with his fathers" is again used in these books beginning with Solomon in 2 Chronicles 9:31. There is no need to list the texts that use this phrase.

The post-exilic books of Ezra and Nehemiah do not add significant content to our study on the issues of the afterlife. The Book of Esther also does not have significant content on the afterlife.

H. A. BAKER

H. A. Baker was the grandfather of Rolland Baker, who is married to Heidi Baker. They have led the amazing mission to orphans and planted congregations in Mozambique, Africa.

H. A. Baker ran an orphanage in Southwest China over ninety years ago from this writing. There was an outpouring of the Spirit on forty of the boys, very young children. Several of these children, who would not have had much biblical information, had amazing visions of heaven, hell, and the heavenly Jerusalem. Independently

15

they described the same thing. If the pictures of hell are taken literally, we have the dilemma that people are not cast into the lake of fire until the last judgment.

> This city in the sky the children saw as three cities in one; one city suspended above another, the largest city below, the smallest city on top, making a pyramid. Since this city John saw is surrounded by a wall, and since the city is one thousand five hundred miles high, Bible students have supposed the heavenly city is not a pyramid but a cube. Our children, however, knew nothing of this, neither had I ever thought of the New Jerusalem as three cities, one suspended above another. God, who suspends the worlds in space, can suspend these cities in space.[1]

> On either side of the beautiful golden streets were buildings side by side, a room for each person, every room opening onto the street. On the door and about the front were precious jewels so resplendently brilliant that the building shone with light and glory. The name of each occupant was above the door.[2]

> In Paradise they saw trees bearing the most delicious fruit, and vistas of the most beautiful flowers of every color, sending forth an aroma of heavenly fragrance. There were birds of glorious plumage singing their carols of joy and praise. In this part were also animals of every size and description; large deer, small deer, large lions, great elephants, lovely rabbits and all sorts of friendly pets such as they had never seen before.[3]

The children saw not only darkness in hell, but also the lake of fire which was always approached through a region of stygian darkness. In vision they were led to the edge of a great lake of molten fire in a semi-dark pit from which arose clouds of smoke. When the smoke settled low, the fire in the lake was less distinct. When the smoke lifted a little, the burning lake with red and greenish flames and its inmates could be distinctly seen.[4]

The lost were seen going into hell. Some fell in, some walked over the brink and some were bound by demon chains and cast into hell by demons. When the fire abated and the smoke settled down, the moans of the miserable could be heard. When the fire at intervals increased in intensity and the smoke lifted a little, there were shrieks and wails of agony.[5]

One boy saw his grandmother in hell. She was once a sorceress and murderer who had withstood the Gospel she heard in her village and caused many to refuse the light. The tribal boy who saw his grandmother in hell was the boy who saw his little sister and his believing aunt in heaven.[6]

Chapter 3

THE POETIC BOOKS AND THE AFTERLIFE

THE BOOK OF JOB

The Book of Job provides limited but important passages on the afterlife. The pessimistic expression during his suffering indicates that Job entertained the idea of death as the cessation of existence.

I note selections from Job 3:12–15, 17–19:

> Why were there knees to receive me and breasts that I might be nursed? For now I would be lying down in peace; I would be at sleep and at rest with kings and rulers of the earth, who built for themselves places now lying in ruins, with princes who had gold, who filled their houses with silver....There the wicked cease from turmoil, and there the weary are at rest. Captives also enjoy their ease; they no longer hear the slave driver's shout. The small and the great are there, and the slaves are freed from their owners.

The sense of leveling in these verses seems to indicate that there is no distinction on the other side of death between the rich and poor, the wicked and righteous, and the slave and master. If so, it appears that text looks toward a complete end.

In Job 14 we read:

> As water disappears from the sea, and a river becomes parched and dries up, so man lies down

and does not rise. Till the heavens are no more, they
will not awake nor be roused from their sleep.

—JOB 14:11–12, NKJV

Yet, Job 19:23–27 has been traditionally interpreted as
one of the most passionate declarations not only on an
afterlife but also in the resurrection from the dead. Yet
there are scholars, especially of a more liberal persuasion,
who do not think that Job could have made such a
declaration.

> Oh, that my words were recorded, that they were
> written on a scroll, that they were inscribed with
> an iron tool on lead, or engraved in rock forever! I
> know that my Redeemer lives, and that in the end
> he will stand upon the earth. And after my skin
> has been destroyed, yet in my flesh I will see God;
> I myself will see him with my own eyes—I, and not
> another. How my heart yearns within me!

The King James Version translates correctly instead
of "skin has been destroyed" as "skin worms destroy this
body." The sense of this may be that the body is fully
destroyed by the worms that eat it. The redeemer could
be God, or we could wonder if Job had some hope in a
Messianic figure. The text even seems to be saying that Job
believed in the resurrection of his body at such a future
time that *in his flesh he would see God.*

However, the other interpretation is that Job was not
talking about a future resurrection but simply his recovery
from the skin disease, worms, and terrible sicknesses that
tried him. He is merely affirming that at the end of this
trial he would see God in some way.

The language itself, however, does lend itself to a hope beyond this life.

THE AFTERLIFE IN THE BOOK OF PSALMS

In the psalms we have the same phenomenon that we find in Job. One psalmist may indicate that death is the end of existence, at least existence in any meaningful sense. Another psalmist may give a strong affirmation of a reward for the righteous after this life. We have to be extremely careful in building doctrine from the psalms. It can indeed and should be done, but we have to sort between those human expressions of the psalmist in prayer and the expressions of faith that fit the developing biblical hope asserted in more didactic passages.

Psalm 6:4–5, for example, states:

> Turn, LORD, and deliver me; save me because of your unfailing love. Among the dead no one proclaims your name. Who praises you from the grave?

This psalmist appeals to God for deliverance so that God will continue to have praise that will cease when he is dead. Other psalms say similar things.

Psalm 49:12–19 is such an important text that it is well to quote it in full:

> People, despite their wealth, do not endure; they are like the beasts that perish. This is the fate of those who trust in themselves, and of their followers, who approve their sayings. They are like sheep and are destined to die; death will be their shepherd (but the upright will prevail over them in the morning). Their forms will decay in the grave, far from their princely mansions. But God will redeem me from

the realm of the dead; he will surely take me to himself. Do not be overawed when others grow rich, when the splendor of their houses increases; for they will take nothing with them when they die, their splendor will not descend with them. Though while they live they count themselves blessed—and people praise you when you prosper—they will join those who have gone before them, who will never again see the light of life. People who have wealth but lack understanding are like the beasts that perish.

One could try to stretch the meanings so that the psalmist is only saying that the rich will eventually perish and then the righteous will rule. The evil rich only have temporary control. However, the psalm is really saying much more and is making some profound truth assertions.

For one thing, the wicked will decay in the grave. There is no clarity about an afterlife for them. There is more than a hint with regard to the phrase that the upright will rule over them in the morning. Is the morning a day of renewal, even resurrection, where the righteous will rule? Of course if the wicked cease to be, ruling over them in the morning only means that the righteous rule and the wicked are dead, or that the righteous rule over their descendants.

Again, there is more in this text. There is a contrast of final destinies. Either cessation of existence or being ruled over by the righteous is the end of the wicked. The wicked are defined as "those who trust in themselves" (v. 13). A life of trusting in God or faith/faithfulness is the key to a good ultimate destiny.

The righteous will be redeemed from the grave. This is without qualification and seems to mean much more than a long life; for as Scripture notes many times, even a long life is short in larger perspective. We read that God will redeem from the grave, and the psalmist says that "he will surely take me to himself" (v. 15).

The conclusion is that the righteous will attain a good final destiny after this life in fellowship with God. There will be a morning for them where they shall rule.

Psalm 72 and the everlasting king

The king of Israel is described in terms that show that he is to fulfill the covenant with Abraham to bless all nations. It says that the king will "endure as long as the sun, as long as the moon, through all generations" (Ps. 72:5).

He will rule to the ends of the earth (v. 8). All kings will bow down to him (v. 11). All nations will be blessed through him (v. 17). The description is so amazing that it is either a super hyperbole (purposive literary exaggeration) or it describes a future permanent Messianic King as in the Book of Isaiah 9:6–7. If the king can be an everlasting figure, it opens the door to others having everlasting life.

Psalm 73, the end of the righteous and the wicked

In Psalm 73 the psalmist uses a literary device by representing himself as questioning the justice of God due to the prosperity of the wicked. In all probability he is representing all people who raise such questions. The description of their self-centered, wicked lives is quite detailed. The psalmist says that it was in vain that he kept his heart pure and washed his hands in innocence (v. 13).

The right understanding came to him when he went into the sanctuary of God. Then he understood their final destiny (v. 17). Final destiny is the topic of this psalm!

The wicked can be suddenly destroyed, and there can be a very quick reversal of circumstances. They will be despised by God as fantasies (v. 20). However, beyond the reversals in this life, there is a judgment beyond death:

> Yet I am always with you; you hold me by my right hand. You guide me with your counsel, and afterward you will take me into glory. Whom have I in heaven but you? And earth has nothing I desire besides you. My flesh and heart may fail, but God is the strength of my heart and my portion forever. Those who are far from you will perish; you destroy all who are unfaithful to you.
>
> —PSALM 73:23–27

There is no thought in this psalm of the wicked continuing in life. It seems that they come to an end. However, the righteous are received by God into glory, in contrast to an end of their existence.

This contrast of final destiny for the wicked and the righteous is important. Certainly the psalmist knows of wicked people who perish in their old age, seemingly not being fully judged in this life for wickedness. How do we describe the righteous, the ones who attain positive final destiny? It is the opposite of the wicked who say, "How can God know? Does the most high have knowledge?" (v. 11). The righteous says that the most high does know indeed, and lives his life in faith/faithfulness in God. The one who will attain a final good destiny trusts in God and is obedient to His standards of righteousness. This will become the consistent orientation of the Hebrew Scriptures. That there must be a way to the forgiveness of sins as part of that obedience is important, but we have not come to those texts yet.

Psalm 88, a more pessimistic expression

We read in verses 10 through 12:

> Do you show your wonders to the dead? Do their
> spirits rise up and praise you? Is your love declared
> in the grave, your faithfulness in Destruction? Are
> your wonders known in the place of darkness, or
> your righteous deeds in the land of oblivion?

Is the grave the underworld of shadowy existence? Most
do think that we should read "the grave" that way. *Sheol*
is not just a literal tomb. Again we find that not all the
psalmists, who in their expressions cry out to God and
bear their souls, were clear on the issue of final destinies.

Psalm 90, the prayer attributed to Moses

The psalmist represents God as saying:

> You turn people back to dust, saying, "Return to
> dust, you mortals." A thousand years in your sight
> are like a day that has just gone by, or like a watch in
> the night. Yet you sweep people away in the sleep of
> death—they are like the new grass of the morning:
> In the morning it springs up new, but by evening it
> is dry and withered.
>
> —Psalm 90:3–6

When we read these words, knowing the content of the
new covenant revelation, we long for the psalmist to say
something more like Psalm 73; but again, the psalm here
is the expression of the psalmist and not necessarily a
doctrinal assertion on the afterlife.

Psalm 116:15

This verse has often been used to show that death is not the end but is a blessing:

> Precious in the sight of the LORD is the death of his saints.
>
> —PSALM 116:15, NKJV

In this case the idea is that this death would not be precious if there was not a fulfillment. Some scholars want to interpret it as "grievous in the sight of the LORD." In both cases the life of the person is precious, but in one because they will come to fulfillment. If the latter is the interpretation, why does God allow or not redeem the person from death if their life coming to an end causes Him pain? We have often heard this verse used in funerals to give comfort to the grieving.

THE BOOK OF PROVERBS

The Book of Proverbs does not provide any clear content on the afterlife. However, there is one text that does not seem capable of fulfillment without a positive destiny after this life. In Proverbs 4:18–19 we read:

> The path of the righteous is like the first gleam of dawn, shining ever brighter till the full light of day. But the path of the wicked is like deep darkness; they do not know what makes them stumble.

Does the phrase "full light of day" imply the idea of a time of glory and power for the righteous in the age to come?

THE BOOK OF ECCLESIASTES

The Book of Ecclesiastes is a compendium of wisdom from a this-worldly perspective. It shows the futility of human life without the perspective of eternity: "'Meaningless! Meaningless!" says the Teacher. "Utterly meaningless! Everything is meaningless" (1:2). The classic translation of *meaningless* as "vanity" is also a good translation.

Note the view of Ecclesiastes 2:24–26:

> A person can do nothing better than to eat and drink and find satisfaction in their own toil. This too, I see, is from the hand of God, for without him, who can eat or find enjoyment? To the person who pleases him, God gives wisdom, knowledge and happiness, but to the sinner he gives the task of gathering and storing up wealth to hand it over to the one who pleases God. This too is meaningless, a chasing after the wind.

Note that the writer, Solomon, in classic understanding, does foster an ethical life as the best way to living through this life; but if death is the end of all things, then it is still ultimately in vain.

There is almost a wrestling with meaning in Ecclesiastes 3:10–14 and 17:

> I have seen the burden God has laid on the human race. He has made everything beautiful in its time. He has also set eternity in the human heart; yet no one can fathom what God has done from beginning to end. I know that there is nothing better for people than to be happy and to do good while they live. That each of them may eat and drink, and find satisfaction in all their toil—this is the gift of God. I

know that everything God does will endure forever; nothing can be added to it and nothing taken from it. God does it so that people will fear him . . . God will bring into judgment both the righteous and the wicked.

If eternity is in their hearts, is he saying that the people want everlasting life? But is this hope to be fulfilled? What God does endures forever; will this include what G. K. Chesterton called *The Everlasting Man*?[1]

Then if God brings the righteous and wicked to judgment, and there is truly a just balancing of the scales of justice, how could it be so if there is no reward and punishment after death? We know that in this life the scales are not nearly balanced. With no life after death, we see the conclusion well laid out in Ecclesiastes 3:18–21:

I also said to myself, "As for humans, God tests them so that they may see that they are like the animals. Surely the fate of human beings is like that of the animals; the same fate awaits them both: As one dies, so dies the other. All have the same breath; humans have no advantage over animals. Everything is meaningless. All go to the same place; all come from dust, and to dust all return. Who knows if the human spirit rises upward and if the spirit of the animal goes down into the earth?"

I believe the point here is that if the spirit of man rises upward, the person continues to be. However, if all end the same way, man and animal, then all is meaningless. There is so much suffering in life that it is better sometimes to have never existed (4:2–3). Such sentiments are repeated in different ways. Righteous men perish in their righteousness and wicked men live long in wickedness (7:15).

Though it is true that it generally goes better for a God-fearing man and for a man who is reverent before God, there are times when it seems that the righteous man gets what the wicked deserve and the wicked get what the righteous deserve (8:12–15). It appears that the righteous and wicked share a common destiny (9:2). The living "know that they will die, but the dead know nothing" (v. 5). They will not "have a part in anything that happens under the sun" (v. 6).

It seems that the book shouts for a reckoning of some kind after death. Is the book a subtle argument for this? The conclusion hints that it is so:

> Here is the conclusion of the matter: Fear God and keep his commandments, for this is the duty of all mankind. For God will bring every deed into judgment, including every hidden thing, whether it is good or evil.
>
> —ECCLESIASTES 12:13–14

If this is so, there has to be life after death for such a judgment to occur, especially in the light of all the other statements about the nature of life if there is no life after death.

THE THOMAS WELCH STORY

Gordon Lindsay, the founder of Christ for the Nations, knew Thomas Welch. This is one of the amazing miracle stories in Christian history. In this story Welch gives his description of his near-death experience.

The story begins with his description of an accident at a lumber mill.

> I fell off the trestle and tumbled down between the timbers and into the pond, which was ten feet deep. An engineer sitting in the cab of his locomotive unloading logs into the pond saw me fall. I landed on my head on the first beam thirty feet down, and then tumbled from one beam to another until I fell into the water and disappeared from his view.... The mill was shut down then and every available man was called to search for my body....The search went on for forty-five minutes to one hour before I was finally found by M. J. H. Gunderson....I was dead as far as this world is concerned. But I was alive in another world....The next thing I knew I was standing near a shoreline of a great ocean of fire. It happened to be what the Bible says it is in Revelation 21:8: "The lake which burneth with fire and brimstone" [KJV]. This is the most awesome sight one could ever see this side of the final judgment. I remember more clearly than any other thing that has ever happened to me in my lifetime every detail of every moment, what I saw and what happened during that hour I was gone from this world. I was standing some distance from this burning, turbulent, rolling mass of blue fire and brimstone. There was nobody in it. I was not in it. I saw other people whom I had known that had died when I was thirteen. Another was a boy I had gone to school with who had died from cancer of the jaw that had started with an infected tooth while he was just a young lad. He was two years older than I. We recognized each other, even though we did not speak. They, too, were looking and seemed to be perplexed and in deep thought, as though they

could not believe what they saw....There is no way to describe it except to say we were eye witnesses now to the final judgment. There is no way to escape, no way out. You don't even try to look for one.[2]

KENNETH HAGIN

The following story is an experience the famous faith healer Kenneth Hagin had as a young teen. He was born in 1917 weighing less than two pounds and with a deformed heart. He was not expected to live. Surviving a sickly childhood, at age fifteen he became totally bedfast, during which time he had a near-death experience.

The following story is his account:

> The farther down I went, the blacker it became, until it was all blackness—I could not have seen my hand if it had been one inch in front of my eyes...
>
> Finally, far below me, I could see lights flickering on the walls of the caverns of the damned. The lights were caused by the fires of hell. The giant, white-crested orb of flame pulled me, drawing me as a magnet draws metal to itself. I did not want to go, but just as metal jumps to the magnet, my spirit was drawn to that place. I could not take my eyes off of it. The heat beat me in the face. Many years have gone by, yet I can see it just as clearly today as I saw it then. It is as fresh in my memory as if it just happened.[3]

Chapter 4

THE PROPHETS

Introduction: Heaven, Hell, and the Afterlife in the Prophets

I think that the best way to do theology is to build from earlier to later texts so we can see the progressive additions to our understanding. We have not absolutely kept to this principle due to the greater ease for most Christians of following the order of the Protestant Bible. Yet, we have mostly followed this orientation. We have already dealt with 1 and 2 Chronicles, though it is a much later book than 1 and 2 Kings that covers much overlapping content. The additions to 1 and 2 Kings on this subject is so limited, we do not believe we have compromised our presentation. Were we to follow chronological order, we would start with Joel and Amos. However, Isaiah is also early, and has such important content that we think we will not much compromise our principle by covering the Major Prophets first.

The category of "major" prophets is due to the length of the books. All were written before or during the Babylonian exile when the Southern Kingdom of Judah was taken captive to Babylon. There is a progression of understanding from Isaiah to Daniel.

Isaiah

The Book of Isaiah presents a vast and wonderful hope for the redemption of Israel and the nations, even the whole world. This vision of world redemption promises a wonderful future *on earth* for those who enter that glorious age to come. A key aspect is that the prophet *does not* look forward to a lasting abode in heaven! He looks forward to redemption of the world and on the earth, though it is described as a new heavens and new earth. The hope is so glorious, the description so wonderful, that a question of justice arises. What about the righteous who died before the arrival of that age? This provides us a context for the hope of Isaiah.

Isaiah lived during the reigns of several kings, beginning with Uzziah and ending with Hezekiah. Two righteous kings frame his ministry, but in between there are wicked kings. The amazing call of Isaiah is recounted in chapter 6. It is in the context of a temple vision. He saw the Lord and tells us that He was seated on the throne and His train or robe filled the temple. He saw angels above the throne whom he calls seraphs. Each had six wings. The description anticipates Ezekiel's vision over one hundred years later. This is a heavenly vision. Heaven is the abode of God Himself and of His angels.

Isaiah writes about terrible judgments to come, including the captivity and scattering of the Northern Tribes and finally of the captivity of the Southern Tribes. Amazingly, in this context, he is given the revelation of the great hope of the restoration of Israel and the redemption of the world.

Isaiah 2 is one of the most well-known passages in the Bible. It speaks of the mountain of the Lord's temple being established as the chief among the mountains. This is in significance, not in height. Then we read:

> Many peoples will come and say, "Come let us go up
> to the mountain of the LORD, to the house of the God

of Jacob. He will teach us his ways, so that we may walk in his paths." The law will go out from Zion, the word of the LORD from Jerusalem. He will judge between the nations and settle disputes for many peoples. They will beat their swords into plowshares and their spears into pruning hooks. Nation will not take up sword against nation, nor will they train for war anymore. Come, O descendants of Jacob, let us walk in the light of the LORD.

—ISAIAH 2:3–5

This vision shows the whole world, all the nations, in unity under the rule of the God of Israel, in obedience to His universal law. The hope is not about going to heaven, but the hope of a new world order brought about by God.

Isaiah 9:6–7 connects this great hope for Israel and the nations to the Messiah, the King who is to come:

For to us a child is born, to us a son is given, and the government will be on his shoulders. And he will be called Wonderful Counselor, Mighty God, Everlasting Father, Prince of Peace. Of the greatness of his government and peace there will be no end. He will reign on David's throne and over his kingdom, establishing and upholding it with justice and righteousness from that time on and forever. The zeal of the Lord Almighty will accomplish this.

This hope comes in the midst of passages about the judgment of God. Again, the hope is not about going to heaven but about a glorious age to come (the Jewish term) upon the earth. It is something that will be brought about by God and His Messiah. We don't know how, but the New Covenant Scriptures will give information on this.

Then in Isaiah 11:1–12 we read a more extensive passage on the same theme. The Messiah is called the shoot that will come up from the stump of Jesse, or a Branch from his roots. Already Isaiah perceives the cutting off of the Davidic dynasty in exile. The dynasty becomes a stump. The Spirit of God will be upon the shoot, upon Him in such a way that His judgments will be supernatural, not of mere human knowledge. He will judge with righteousness for the poor of the earth but will also strike the earth with what Isaiah calls the rod of His mouth. He will slay the wicked by the breath of His lips.

The effect of His work will be a change in nature itself, for the wolf will live with the lamb, and the leopard with the goat. Even poisonous snakes will not be a danger. Children will play with them with no danger. The lion will eat straw.

The climatic statement is in verse 9:

> They will neither harm nor destroy on all my holy mountain, for the earth will be filled with the knowledge of the Lord as the waters cover the sea.

The passage thus envisions the worldwide knowledge of God; being filled with the Spirit is also being filled with knowledge. This is also a day in which the children of Israel will be re-gathered.

Again, the hope is a glorious age on earth, not about going to heaven. This idea of a glorious age is again in view in Isaiah 25 where the mountain of the Lord (Zion) provides a great banquet of rich food for all people (v. 6). The shroud over all people will be removed (v. 7). He will wipe away the tears from all eyes and remove the disgrace of His people from the earth, and He will swallow up death forever (v. 8). But how does this help those who already died? The Isaiah 25 text does not speak of the solution for them. However, if there are no tears, can it be that the prophet envisions the end of death?

Isaiah 26 indeed makes an important contribution to our understanding of the ultimate end. The context is the disappointment that Israel has not fulfilled her destiny to bring the nations to birth into the Kingdom. She only gave birth to wind and not to the people of the world. We read in verse 19:

> But your dead will live, Lord; their bodies will rise—
> let those who dwell in the dust wake up and shout
> for joy—your dew is like the dew of the morning;
> the earth will give birth to her dead.

This will follow the severe judgments of the nations prophesied in verses 20 and 21.

The prophet then presents the marvelous revelation from God that the reality of the age to come is only wonderful if the righteous are raised from the dead to participate in it. This text is foundational for the doctrine of the Resurrection and Judaism and Christianity. Our destiny in the afterlife is not as ethereal souls floating around but as fully physical human beings, but without the limitations of sickness and death.

In Isaiah 38 King Hezekiah responds to a miraculous healing and God's granting him fifteen more years of life (v. 5). As we noted in the psalms, the idea of death leading to a shadowy, undesirable existence is reflected in his poetic response in verse 18:

> For the grave cannot praise you, death cannot sing
> your praise; those who go down to the pit cannot
> hope for your faithfulness.

We again find that sometimes the expression of a biblical personage is not the same as a doctrinal assertion by another writer.

Isaiah 65 presents an interesting dilemma. It presents the age to come as living a long time and not the end of death as in Isaiah 25 or a day of resurrection as in Isaiah 26. There is no systematic harmonization in the book. Isaiah speaks of a "new heavens and a new earth" (Isa. 65:17) where the former things will not be remembered— that is the painful former times. We read that the sound of weeping and crying will no longer be heard in Jerusalem (v. 19). Then we read in verse 20:

> Never again will there be in it an infant who lives
> but a few days, or an old man who does not live
> out his years; the one who dies at a hundred will be
> thought a mere child; the one who fails to reach a
> hundred will be considered accursed.

Then in verse 22 it says, "For as the days of a tree, so will be the days of my people." The picture here is of people living a very long time. One hundred is the age of a youth. The age of a tree can be hundreds of years. Could this be the restoration of pre-flood longevity? Yet if others are resurrected to live in this age, do they die again? Would this wipe away tears from all eyes if all just die again?

The resolution to this in both Judaism and Christianity is to point to a millennial age where people live a very long time but also an everlasting age to follow where people live forever. The term "new heavens and new earth" here is taken by premillennial Christians to not refer to the ultimate new heavens and earth as in Revelation 21:1. Rather it is a glorious but interim age where resurrected people participate in a transitional age and live a very long time but still die, but to be resurrected at the final judgment (Rev. 20:11–15). Those who were resurrected for this age do not die again. We will look at these passages as part of our New Testament interpretation. Those who do not believe in a real millennial age take this passage as symbolic of everlasting life, but I cannot see any reason to not take this passage straightforwardly.

DANIEL

The Book of Daniel is the next book that speaks of the afterlife, though it is not a primary emphasis of the book. As other prophetic books, it concentrates on the condition of the corporate nation of Israel on this earth. Similar to the Isaiah 26 resurrection passage, Daniel looks to a time of great distress in the world. The text is quite amazing:

> Multitudes who sleep in the dust of the earth will awake; some to everlasting life and others to shame and everlasting contempt. Those who are wise will shine like the brightness of the heavens, and those who lead many to righteousness, like the stars for ever and ever.
>
> —DANIEL 12:2–3

This text on the resurrection is parallel to the later text in Revelation 20. We have a clear indication that the state of the person after a final judgment is permanent. There is no universalism (the idea that all will eventually be saved) in the passage. A bodily resurrection to everlasting life for the righteous is declared. They shine forever like stars. What is the nature of everlasting contempt? We are not told. Is it conscious suffering in a state cut off from God, or is it the memory of their judgment or their experience of their judgment? There seems to be a sense of eternal suffering. The experience of being contemptible is a frightening prospect, though we are given no details.

This ends our study of the Hebrew Bible on this topic.

RAYMOND MOODY

Raymond Moody wrote what has become a classic in the movement of people who believe in the afterlife on the evidence of near-death experiences, first asserted by the psychiatrist Elisabeth Kübler-Ross. Some evangelicals have been disturbed by the fact that in Moody and other writers almost everyone has a positive experience who remembers a near-death experience. This does present a problem on the basis of the biblical evidence. Moody and others provide many experiences like the one below:

> The next thing I knew it seemed as if I were on a ship or small vessel sailing at the other side of a large body of water. On the distant shore, I could see all of my loved ones who had died—my mother, my father, my sister, and others. I could see them, could see their faces, just as they were when I knew them on earth. They seemed to be beckoning me to come on over. Beyond the midst, I could see people, and their forms were just like they are on earth, and I could also see something which one could take to be buildings. The whole thing was permeated with the most gorgeous light—a living, golden, yellow glow, a pale color, not like the harsh gold color we know on earth.[1]

MAURICE RAWLINGS

I consider Maurice Rawlings's book to be the most important written on life after death based on near-death experiences. Maurice Rawlings was a specialist in internal medicine and cardiovascular diseases at the Diagnostic Hospital in Chattanooga, Tennessee. He had many times resuscitated patients who had cardiac arrest, some who were without heartbeat for so long that they were as if dead. They had NDEs, or near-death experiences, that are today part of common cultural information. Usually these people who have been the subjects of such reports went to something like heaven. Rawlings revived people who had an experience of hell. Rawlings theorized that the experience of hell was so terrible that if a patient was not debriefed immediately after resuscitation, he would forget the experience and suppress it. Rawlings made a practice to ask his patients if they experienced anything while they were being resuscitated.

One patient who had an attack on a treadmill test was revived and then relapsed many times.

> Each time he regained heartbeat and respiration, the patient screamed, "I am in hell!" He was terrified and pleaded with me to help him. I was scared to death....He then issued a very strange plea: "Don't stop!"...Most patients when they recover consciousness say, "Take your hands off my chest, you're hurting me."...I noticed a terrified look worse than the expression seen in death! This patient had a grotesque grimace expressing shear horror! His pupils were dilated, and he was perspiring and trembling—he looked as if his hair was "on end."...Then still another strange thing

happened. He said, "Don't you understand? I am in hell. Each time you quit, I go back to hell! Don't let me go back to hell."[2]

Following is an account of a woman who was struck by lightning on a camping trip:

"At the moment that I was hit, I knew exactly what had happened to me. My mind was crystal clear. I had never been so totally alive as in the act of dying." (Regrets of past actions together with things she wanted to do with her life filled her mind.)..."At this point in the act of dying, I had what I call the answer to a question I had never verbalized to anyone or even faced: Is there really a God? I can't describe it, but the totality and reality of the living God exploded within my being and He filled every atom of my body with His glory. In the next moment, to my horror, I found that I wasn't going toward God. I was going away from Him. It was like seeing what might have been, but going away from it. In my panic, I started trying to communicate with the God I knew was there." She begged for her life and offered it to God would he spare it. She recovered fully in three months.[3]

The following is another account:

During this coma, I found myself floating in a valley. There was a light in the distance on a mountain and as I approached the mountain, I noticed beautiful orchids and flowers growing on its rocky slope. Among the boulders I saw my grandfather standing. He had been dead several years. I didn't talk to him but I knew I wanted to stay and I didn't want to come back.[4]

Another account says:

There was a river below me, and it was becoming dawn. Everything was getting brighter. I noticed that I was crossing over a beautiful city below, as I followed the river like a soaring bird. The streets seemed to be made of shining gold and were wonderfully beautiful. I can't describe it. I descended into one of the streets and people were all around me—happy people who were glad to see me! They seemed to be in shining clothes with a sort of glow. Nobody was in a hurry. Some other people were coming toward me. I think they were my parents. But then I woke up, back in my hospital room.[5]

Another account tells us:

After soaring for a while, the angel set me down on a street in a fabulous city of buildings made of glittering gold and silver and beautiful trees. A beautiful light was everywhere—glowing but not bright enough to make me squint my eyes. On this street I met my mother, my father and my brother, all of whom had died previously.... "Here comes Paul," I heard my mother say. As I walked to greet them, however, this same angel picked me up by the waist again and took me off into the sky. I didn't know they wouldn't let me stay.... In the distance we were approaching the skyline. I could recognize the buildings. I saw the hospital where I had been as a patient [and] didn't know where I had been. The angel descended and put me back in the very room where I had been sent as a patient.[6]

PART II

THE NEW COVENANT AND THE AFTERLIFE

Chapter 5

THE SYNOPTIC GOSPELS
AND THE AFTERLIFE

THERE IS A wealth of material on the afterlife in the New Testament, much more than we find in the much more extensive canon of the Hebrew Bible. We begin our survey with the Gospels. In this we have a choice. While most scholars believe that Mark was the first written Gospel, most readers begin reading the New Testament with Matthew. Though scholars believe that Matthew and Luke incorporated much of Mark, we think for our purposes that using the canonical order of the New Testament as we have it makes it simpler for the ordinary reader. We will not repeat parallel texts from Mark and Luke unless they provide additional information. As we go through the foundational texts on our subject, we will ask questions of the text before drawing a conclusion. Often people read their assumptions or the views of their teachers into the text and think the text says more than it says.

THE GOSPEL OF MATTHEW

Matthew 6 speaks about treasures in heaven:

> Do not lay up for yourselves treasures on earth, where moth and rust destroy and where thieves

> break in and steal; but lay up for yourselves treasures
> in heaven, where neither moth nor rust destroy and
> where thieves do not break in and steal. For where
> your treasure is, there your heart will be also.
> —Matthew 6:19–21, nkjv

By the time of Yeshua, the Pharisees were teaching the doctrine of the resurrection and that the righteous would be raised from the dead to participate in the age to come. Everlasting life was an established doctrine among them. New Testament texts show that Yeshua and Paul agreed with the Pharisees on this doctrine (Matt. 22:29–32; Acts 23:6). The idea of resurrection included rewards and punishments in the age to come. Yeshua's teaching on treasures in heaven called His followers to the everlasting blessings through the kind of good works that would bring everlasting fruit and would be a source of rejoicing forever. That fruit is our effect on the lives of people who through our works can discover the way of life lived in the power of love.

In Matthew 7:21–23, Yeshua speaks of a separation between hypocrites and His true followers:

> Not everyone who says to me, "Lord, Lord," will
> enter the kingdom of heaven, but only he who
> does the will of my Father who is in heaven. Many
> will say to me on that day, "Lord, Lord, did we not
> prophesy in your name, and in your name drive out
> demons and perform many miracles?" Then I will
> tell them plainly, "I never knew you. Away from me,
> you evildoers."

In the first three Gospels (the Synoptic Gospels), the Kingdom of God is presented as a present reality to be embraced and entered into. The Kingdom is also presented as something yet future to come in fullness or the age to come that begins after the time of the return of Yeshua. In this text the future dimension of the Kingdom is in view. The Lord will tell them to depart. Is this forever? What kind of life will be lived by those who are in this category of those who are told to depart? We are not told. However, there is clearly something terrible to be avoided. The judgment here is not about a universal judgment for all people. It is a judgment of individuals in Israel who did not commit themselves to do the will of God and are not real disciples but pretenders. Pretenders can even do miracles!

In Matthew 10 Yeshua sends out the twelve to announce the good news of the Kingdom. They are to "heal the sick, raise the dead, cleanse those who have leprosy, drive out demons" (v. 8). Those who do not listen to them will be severely judged. The power revealed is so great that apparently they are without excuse. So Yeshua says, "It will be more bearable for Sodom and Gomorrah on the day of judgment than for that town" (v. 15). This presents us with the question of how the final judgment can be bearable in any sense unless it is limited. Or are we looking at levels of punishment in hell? Others look at a purgatorial meaning; a temporary hell judgment that comes to an end but in an eventual final good end. Others argue that the tolerable judgment has to do with the fact that the person will cease to be after more or less severe suffering. Why is there so much debate? Because the passage just does not give us clarity about the final judgment and the state of the lost.

In Matthew 10:28 Yeshua presents the idea that God can destroy both body and soul in hell. The context is part of exhortations to courage to stand firm in difficulties and persecutions. In verse 22 Yeshua states that the one who stands firm to the end will be saved. I take this to be in the context of the hope of the resurrection. Verse 28 says:

> Do not be afraid of those who kill the body but cannot kill the soul. Rather, be afraid of the One who can destroy both soul and body in hell.

In addition Yeshua follows up this exhortation with the encouragement that not a sparrow falls to the ground without the knowledge of the Father; even the hairs of our heads are numbered, and we are of much more worth than sparrows (vv. 29–31). The resurrection therefore is the ultimate hope of those who stand firm in loyalty to Yeshua.

The person continues to live after the body is destroyed. However, God can destroy both body and soul, and He alone is to be feared. Those who argue that the final destiny of those who are ultimately judged as unrighteous is total annihilation use this text for support. Total annihilation certainly fits this text. However, the text does not say that God will totally annihilate the unrighteous, but that He can do this; it is within His power. We will have to look at many other texts on this issue.

In Matthew 10:42 we read that there is a reward for anyone who gives a cup of cold water to a little one who is a disciple of Yeshua. Receiving a righteous man brings a righteous man's reward (v. 41). These texts raise interesting questions about who is part of a good destiny in the life beyond or the nature of the reward. Any consignment to an everlasting hell of pain and judgment cannot be considered connected to a positive reward. How broad is the hope of a good end in the age to come? Again, many more texts will have to be considered.

Matthew 11:20–24 records the denunciation of the cities in which Yeshua performed His miracles but they did not repent. He predicts destruction for these cities, which later occurred in the war against Rome (AD 66–70). However, two verses have special significance for our study. Verse 22 says, "It will be more bearable for Tyre and Sidon on the day of judgment than for you." Then He pronounces judgment on Capernaum and says in verse 24: "But I tell you that it will be more bearable for Sodom on the day of judgment than for you."

This seems to be speaking about a future judgment for all these towns: Tyre, Sidon, and Sodom—pagan towns; and Capernaum, Bethsaida, and Korizon—Jewish towns. So three cities of pagans will have a more tolerable judgment than the three Jewish towns. Can everlasting punishment in hell be described as more or less tolerable? Traditional theology spoke of different levels of punishment in hell, but in what sense would be it more or less tolerable? Or is this punishment of limited duration but a duration determined according to deserts? These alternatives have been argued. My view is that the passage leaves us without clarity for answering these questions, but the passages are giving a very serious warning of something terrible.

One of the most important passages in the Bible on final judgment is found in Matthew 12:31–32.

> And so I tell you, every kind of sin and slander can
> be forgiven, but blasphemy against the Spirit will
> not be forgiven. Anyone who speaks a word against
> the Son of Man will be forgiven, but anyone who

speaks against the Holy Spirit will not be forgiven, either in this age or in the age to come.

There has been disagreement in interpretation, but there is a majority consensus that I believe is probably correct. The context of the passage is the accusation of the Pharisees against Yeshua—that He was driving out demons by the power of Beelzebub, the prince of demons. Yeshua claimed that this would be contrary to Satan's purposes and would be a kingdom divided against itself. Satan is not in the business of freeing people from his power. In addition, Yeshua said, "But if I drive out demons by the Spirit of God, then the kingdom of God has come upon you" (v. 28).

The Pharisees attributed the work of the Holy Spirit to the devil, and this was blasphemy. But why the contrast whereby one can be forgiven for speaking against the Son of Man but not for speaking against the Spirit? There are many examples of Christians and Messianic Jews not discerning the work of the Holy Spirit and speaking negatively. So there must be something deeper. I think, as do many commentators, that the issue is the context of the Spirit working on the hearts of the people who witness the work of the Spirit. It is the Spirit that convicts the heart and brings the person to respond to the good news. In that context, to reject the work of the conviction of the Spirit in the context of seeing the work of the Spirit, places the person in great jeopardy since they reject the only one who can bring a person into right relationship to God. If one speaks against the Son, it can be a mere human wrong evaluation. When the Spirit is working, however, we are dealing with something different. It is knowledge by heart conviction and has to be accepted or resisted. The pronouncement of Yeshua is one of the clearest statements about ultimate condemnation. It appears that a person can reject the work of the Spirit in an irrevocable way. He is then "not forgiven, either in this age or in the age to come" (v. 32). This seems like a permanent irrevocable and everlasting judgment.

Matthew 12:41-42 speaks in parallel to Matthew 11:20–24, whereby those from pagan nations will condemn those in Israel who did not respond rightly to the work of the Spirit.

> The men of Nineveh will stand up at the judgment with this generation and condemn it; for they repented at the preaching of Jonah, and now something greater than Jonah is here. The Queen of the South will rise at the judgment with this generation and condemn it; for she came from the ends of the earth to listen to Solomon's wisdom, and now something greater than Solomon is here.

In this case, contrary to those in the Matthew 11 passage, the pagans repented and the Queen of Sheba received Solomon's wisdom. What will that judgment be? We are not told in this passage, but the warning is severe.

The idea of final judgment is also taught in the parables of Yeshua. In the parable of the weeds in Matthew 13:24–30, a man sowed good seed and an enemy came and sowed weeds among the wheat. Both sprouted together. When the servants asked about pulling up the weeds, the owner said to wait so that pulling the weeds would not uproot the wheat. Then at the harvest the weeds would be collected first and tied in bundles to be burned, and the wheat would be gathered into the barn.

It is clear from the Jewish context of that day that Yeshua is noting that in society wheat (people of God) and weeds (people of evil and influenced by the evil one) will grow together until the end of this age. Eventually there will be a final harvest and separation. Yeshua interprets the parable just as we would have expected in verses 37 through 43. The good seed is sown by the Son of Man (Yeshua) and the weeds are the sons of the evil one, and sown by the devil. At the end of the age those who do evil will be gathered and thrown "into the fiery furnace where there will be weeping and gnashing of teeth" (v. 42). The righteous on the other hand will shine like the sun in the kingdom of the Father. This is a parallel to the text in Daniel 12.

The parable teaches that there will be a final separation of the wicked from the righteous. The wicked will enter a realm spoken of as a place of suffering or a fiery furnace. How long does this last? When the weeds are burned do they cease to be? That is generally the case with literal weeds. Is Yeshua saying that this burning lasts forever, or does it lead to the final ceasing of the people who are so judged? There is significant debate over this question.

The parable of the net in verses 47 through 50 is similar. A net is let down into the lake and the fishermen catch all kinds of fish. When it is pulled to shore, the fishermen sort the fish. The good is put in baskets but the bad are thrown away. Yeshua interprets this parable to state that at the end of the age the angels will separate the wicked from the righteous. Again we are told in the same language that the wicked will be thrown "into the fiery furnace where there will be weeping and gnashing of teeth" (v. 50). We are left with the same two possibilities from this parable: either terrible temporary suffering and then being consumed or coming to an end, or continued existence in a place of terrible suffering. Whatever interpretation we choose, the end of the wicked is terrible and is more than just ceasing to be at death. A fearful judgment awaits the wicked.

In Matthew 16 Yeshua exhorts His disciples that anyone who would come after Him "must deny himself and take up his cross and follow me" (v. 24). Those who seek to save their lives will lose their lives, and those who lose them for Yeshua will save them (v. 25). Yeshua is here speaking of more than the quality and worth of the normal course of a human life, for He continues with the words: "What good will it be for a man if he gains the whole world, yet forfeits his soul? Or what can a man give in exchange for his soul?" (v. 26). Finally we end with these words, "For the Son of man is going to come in his Father's glory with his angels, and then he will reward each person according to what he has done" (v. 27).

The Bible is quite clear that there will be differences in rewards and punishments according to the good or evil works of the person who is judged. Other texts have to be appealed to for whether a foundation for a good end is embracing Yeshua—and there are many such texts. The totality of how a person lives is the consistent basis in Scripture for rewards and punishment, while embracing Yeshua in response to the good news is considered the act above all others that places one in right relationship with God. However, a person who has embraced Yeshua is a person who brings forth good works.

Warnings of the possibility of severe judgment after death or at the time of universal judgment at the end of this age are common in the teaching of Yeshua. The idea that He only taught the love of God in such a way that everything would be resolved in a positive way for all people just does not fit the numerous texts of the Bible. Here is another such text.

> And whoever welcomes one such child in my name welcomes me. If anyone causes one of these little ones—those who believe in me—to stumble, it would be better for them to have a large millstone hung around their neck and to be drowned in the depths of the sea. Woe to the world because of the things that cause people to stumble! Such things must come, but woe to the person through whom they come! If your hand or your foot causes you to stumble, cut it off and throw it away. It is better for you to enter life maimed or crippled than to have two hands or two feet and be thrown into eternal fire. And if your eye causes you to stumble, gouge it out and throw it away. It is better for you to enter life with one eye than to have two eyes and be thrown into the fire of hell.
>
> —MATTHEW 18:5–9

Note the basis for judgment in the first section is causing a child to sin. The judgment for such an act must be quite severe if it would be better for a millstone to be hung around the person's neck and for him to be thrown into the sea.

In the second section, Yeshua counsels to cut off a hand or to pluck out an eye rather than to be captured by sin through sight (lust for possessions or sexual desire) or by the use of one's hands (like in stealing). If one lives in sin, their destiny is to be cast into eternal fire. Most scholars think that a literary method of exaggerated language is used by Yeshua to make His point. However, one scholar of note did think Yeshua was speaking literally concerning cutting off one's hand and gouging out the eye. Of course, through the power of God, all can overcome sin; so the necessity to cut off a hand and gouge out an eye is hypothetical. The point remains that a terrible judgment awaits those who engage in and practice serious sin. The word *eternal* is used. In the history of the Church this was taken to mean that the damned would suffer eternally in hellfire. Others have pointed out that the fire is eternal; but the passage does not say that the suffering of the damned is everlasting. Eternal fire can connote the finality of the judgment.

Another promise of a glorious future in the age to come for Yeshua's followers is found in Matthew 19:28–30:

> Truly I tell you, at the renewal of all things, when the Son of Man sits on his glorious throne, you who have followed me will also sit on twelve thrones, judging the twelve tribes of Israel. And everyone who has left houses or brothers or sisters or father or mother or wife or children or fields for my sake will receive a hundred times as much and will inherit eternal life. But many who are first will be last, and many who are last will be first.

It is interesting to note the very Jewish or Israelite-ish nature of the promise for the twelve disciples: that they will rule over the nation of Israel in the age to come. The nation of Israel thus continues in the age to come. Then there is a promise to all who truly follow Yeshua and leave both possessions and family for the sake of Yeshua. They will receive a hundred times more in the age to come. This, again, is a promise of reward. Everlasting life is promised to them.

In Matthew 22:1–14 we read the parable of the wedding

banquet of a king. Many are invited to the wedding, but they do not come. So the king sends his servants to the street corners and invites any who will come. They gathered both good and bad people. Obviously the parable is about the invitation into the Kingdom of God. In Matthew the Kingdom of God is a present and future reality. When one embraces the gospel, he or she enters the realm of the Kingdom and lives in and from it. However, the experience of the fullness of the Kingdom awaits the return of Yeshua. So what interests us is the possible implication for the afterlife of verses 11–14.

> But when the king came in to see the guests, he noticed a man there who was not wearing wedding clothes. He asked, "How did you get in here without wedding clothes, friend?" The man was speechless. Then the king told the attendants, "Tie him hand and foot, and throw him outside, into the darkness, where there will be weeping and gnashing of teeth." For many are invited, but few are chosen.

The same language is repeated as in Matthew 13:42 on weeping and the gnashing of teeth, so the passage is speaking about the final judgment. The wedding banquet is the ultimate Kingdom. So who is this one who is not properly clothed? It has been quite easy for Christians to teach that we have to be clothed with His righteousness and covered by His blood atonement; that this is the garment needed. The garment that does not qualify is works of righteousness. However, this is reading into the text, though we do have other texts that teach these things. Yet, still other texts teach that we have to be clothed with sincerity and truth.

The issue in Matthew is that religious leaders refuse to

come, but some seek to enter who are false professors of faith. Many are called; but those chosen, who are allowed entrance, have to be genuine. I think the best context for this section is Matthew 7:21–23:

> Not everyone who says "Lord, Lord," will enter the kingdom of heaven, but only he who does the will of my Father who is in heaven. Many will say to me on that day, "Lord. Lord, did we not prophesy in your name, and in your name drive out demons and perform many miracles?" Then I will tell them plainly, "I never knew you. Away from me…!"

So who is the person unclothed? It is the one who does not come in genuine repentance, turning his heart to the Lord. It is the one who is a hypocrite. They are called but cannot be chosen. As in Matthew 7, they try to come to the wedding feast but they cannot get in.

In Matthew 22:23–24 Yeshua responds to the objection of the Sadducees to the doctrine of the resurrection. The Sadducees present a situation where a man died without children, so the woman becomes the wife of a brother to fulfill the Law of Moses to raise an heir in the brother's name. Yet she has no children by this brother, who dies. Then she is married to a third, a fourth, and finally to a seventh. None of them can produce a child with her. So the Sadducees ask whose wife she will be in the resurrection. Yeshua responds that they have a crude idea of the resurrection. In this important text Yeshua says:

> You are in error because you do not know the Scriptures or the power of God. At the resurrection people will neither marry nor be given in marriage; they will be like the angels in heaven. But about the

resurrection of the dead—have you not read what
God said to you? "I am the God of Abraham, the
God of Isaac, and the God of Jacob"? He is not the
God of the dead but of the living.

—MATTHEW 22:29–32

Yeshua here clearly affirms the resurrection of the body
as our ultimate state of existence in the age to come, but
it is a different kind of body that will not be sexually
oriented. For today's society, fulfillment without sexual
fulfillment is disappointing since there is such an idolatry
of sexuality; but the greatest of pleasures will be in love,
fellowship, creativity, and beauty experienced with God
and others.

In the parable of the ten virgins in Matthew 25:1–13,
ten virgins are invited to be part of the wedding party
that will go to meet the bridegroom for the wedding
festivities. Jewish weddings followed a tradition where the
bridegroom would come for his bride, but sometimes as a
surprise. So those who wanted to be part of the festivities
would have to be ready. Five made preparation with
adequate oil for their lamps in case of a delay, but five did
not. The bridegroom came at midnight, and the virgins
who did not make adequate preparation were not able to
buy oil in time. By the time they arrived at the wedding
banquet, the door was shut. They begged for the door to
be open, but he replied, "I tell you the truth, I don't know
you" (v. 12). The moral is to "therefore keep watch, because
you do not know the day or the hour" (v. 13).

Is the exclusion an everlasting judgment or an exclusion
to be part of the higher place of celebration when the age
to come begins? The idea seems to be that people not
be ill prepared. Does this imply falling away due to the

delay? At any rate, faithfulness is here taught as a key to entering into the wedding feast. Living a life on the basis of constant readiness is a foundation of our spiritual life and for avoiding judgment.

In Matthew 25:14–30 we read the parable of the talents. Three servants are given talents (an amount of money). One is given five, the second two, and the last one. The first two invest the money and double it. The last one buries it and only returns the one talent. The first two are rewarded with responsibilities "to be in charge of many things" (vv. 21, 23). The last one, however, is rebuked. His talent is taken from him and given to the first servant. Then we are told:

> For whoever has will be given more, and they will have an abundance. Whoever does not have, even what they have will be taken from them. And throw that worthless servant outside, into the darkness, where there will be weeping and gnashing of teeth.
> —Matthew 25:29–30

Once again we meet with this by now familiar language: "outer darkness where there will be weeping and gnashing of teeth." This is more than not being given as much of a reward. Rather, it seems to be a final destiny. Does it last forever? Is it destruction or everlasting suffering? The text does not indicate an end to the weeping and gnashing of teeth nor does it explicitly say it is everlasting.

Then Matthew 25:31–46 presents another parable about the judgment of the sheep and goats. We read that "all the nations will be gathered before him, and he will separate the people one from another as a shepherd separates the sheep from the goats" (v. 32).

Some teach that this is a separation of nations with

regard to their treatment of the Jewish people, whereas others teach that it is about the treatment of the needy in general. The subject of need is "the least of these brothers of mine" (v. 40). The phrase can easily be taken in both ways.

The basis of the ultimate judgment in this passage is the treatment of these needy ones. The King says to the sheep on the right, "Come, you who are blessed by my Father; take your inheritance, the kingdom prepared for you since the creation of the world" (v. 34). This is the everlasting Kingdom, the Kingdom in fullness. The King gives reason for their blessed final end:

> For I was hungry and you gave me something to eat, I was thirsty and you gave me something to drink, I was a stranger and you invited me in, I needed clothes and you clothed me, I was sick and you looked after me, I was in prison and you came to visit me.
>
> —Matthew 25:35–36

The blessed ones ask when they did these things, and Yeshua states that when they did this to the least of His brethren, they did it for Him (v. 40). Even so, those who are judged and lost are those who did not do these things and they are said to have not done it for Yeshua. The conclusion is quite alarming: "Then they will go away to eternal punishment, but the righteous to eternal life" (v. 46).

Is this final judgment eternal by quality? Does the judgment last forever, never being reversed? Is it everlasting suffering or the punishment of eventually ceasing to be? These are the debates of our day.

MARK AND LUKE AND FINAL DESTINIES

We will not repeat material from Mark and Luke where the same material has been adequately covered from Matthew. We will only add where there is a significant addition.

In Mark 8:34–38 we find a parallel passage to Matthew and Luke where Yeshua tells the disciples that those who would follow Him must take up their cross and follow Him: "Whoever wants to save his life will lose it" (v. 35). In Mark this is applied to being ashamed of Yeshua; that is, keeping silent about alignment with Yeshua or denying that one is a follower of Yeshua and to thereby avoid persecution and save one's own life. Yeshua concludes in verse 38:

> If anyone is ashamed of me and my words in this adulterous and sinful generation, the Son of Man will be ashamed of him when he comes in his Father's glory with the holy angels.

The text does not say that the person will be forever lost but that they at last will have to face the Son of Man and His disappointment over their seeking to save their life and not profess their connection to Yeshua.

In Mark 16:16 we read, "Whoever believes and is baptized will be saved, but whoever does not believe will be condemned."

Luke records the promise of Yeshua to those who are hated, excluded, and insulted because of their connection to Yeshua (the Son of Man). He says, "Rejoice in that day and leap for joy, because great is your reward in heaven. For that is how their fathers treated the prophets" (6:23). The teaching of Yeshua is consistent in asserting that there are levels of both reward and punishment at the judgment.

In the parables of the faithful servants in Luke 12:35–48, we find three related parables. The first tells the story of servants who faithfully wait for their master to return from a wedding banquet. They are ready no matter what the hour (the watch in the night). It will be good for those who are watching when the master comes. The master, contrary to normal practice, will dress himself and wait on his servants! This seems to show the love and care of Yeshua for those who served Him with watchfulness. To most commentators it is connected to ultimate judgment and the return of the Lord. Immediately Yeshua adds another short parable about an owner of the house who, if he knew what hour the thief was coming, would prevent a break-in. So again, the exhortation is to watch, for as Yeshua says, "The Son of Man will come at an hour when you do not expect him" (v. 40). Living in readiness, watching, is a key to a good reward in the afterlife.

In response to Peter's question about to whom Yeshua speaks, Yeshua gives an answer for all. This third short parable is about the faithful and wise manager:

> Who then is the faithful and wise manager, whom the master puts in charge of his servants to give them their food allowance at the proper time? It will be good for that servant whom the master finds doing so when he returns. Truly I tell you, he will put him in charge of all his possessions. But suppose the servant says to himself, "My master is taking a long time in coming," and he then begins to beat the other servants, both men and women, and to eat and drink and get drunk. The master of that servant will come on a day when he does not expect him

and at an hour he is not aware of. He will cut him to pieces and assign him a place with the unbelievers.

—Luke 12:42–46

We could ask if this parable is about the leader's faithfulness. It looks to the return of Yeshua, which may have not been clearly understood at the time of Yeshua's delivery (His death, resurrection, and second coming were not clearly understood until after His ascension). At His return, unfaithful leaders will be condemned to a negative final destiny; that is to a place with unbelievers.

The teaching on the narrow door is a significant passage on the afterlife or life in the age to come. Yeshua responds to the question of whether there would be only a few people saved:

> Make every effort to enter through the narrow door, because many, I tell you, will try to enter and will not be able to. Once the owner of the house gets up and closes the door, you will stand outside knocking and pleading, "Sir, open the door for us." But he will answer, "I don't know you or where you come from." Then you will say, "We ate and drank with you, and you taught in our streets." But he will reply, "I don't know you or where you come from. Away from me, all you evildoers!" There will be weeping there, and gnashing of teeth, when you see Abraham, Isaac, and Jacob and all the prophets in the kingdom of God, but you yourselves thrown out. People will come from the east and west and north and south, and will take their places at the feast in the kingdom of God. Indeed, there are those who are last who will be first, and first who will be last.
>
> —Luke 13:24–30

There are important points in this text. A good final destiny is connected to entering a narrow door. This means a choice for a godly life. Those who do not make this narrow door choice claim a connection to Yeshua, but He responds that He never knew them. The final destiny of those who are righteous is to see the patriarchs and the prophets and to join them in the great feast of the Kingdom of God, the Kingdom in its fullness. The age to come is described in the Bible as a glorious and concrete existence, a bodily life in a totally renewed earth. People will come from the east and west, north and south to be part of this banquet. That the last will be first and the first last in some cases shows that those who have perceived status at the time are really not righteous or so far ahead, so a great reversal will take place. Those who are invited and enter through repentance will attain that destiny as we have seen in other texts from Matthew.

Those who are excluded from this destiny are said to weep and gnash their teeth, the familiar phrase repeated in other texts. This phrase is common in the teaching of Yeshua to describe the danger of a very awful destiny in the afterlife.

In Luke 14:13–14 Yeshua counsels His followers to invite the poor, the crippled and lame, and the blind. They cannot repay, but those who do this will be repaid at the resurrection of the righteous. Here again, the final destiny of the righteous in the age to come is to attain a bodily resurrection and a glorious, desirable, everlasting life.

Verses 15 through 23 continue the same theme as the banquet. Many who were invited refuse to come. We covered this parable in Matthew. However, the concluding words are a bit different. We read the words of the master: "I tell you, not one of these men who were invited will get a taste of my banquet" (v. 24). If the banquet is the symbol of the everlasting life of the righteous in the age to come—and this is a very good probability—then the exclusion would seem to be as lasting as the banquet. He does not say that they will taste it after paying a long price in purgatory, but that they will not taste it. This seems to be indicating finality.

The story of the rich man and Lazarus in Luke 16:19-31 is important. It is debated as to whether or not this is a parable or a historical account, but on either score the basic message is the same. The passage reflects a Jewish view at the time that until the coming of the Messiah and the age to come, those who have died are held in a place of waiting. Pharisaic Judaism, based on the prophets, taught that the righteous would be resurrected to participate in the age to come. There was also an established view of the judgment of the righteous and the wicked at this future time, as taught in Daniel 12, which was a very influential passage in the first century. The rich man obviously lives a selfish life and does not use his wealth to relieve the sufferings of the poor. He ends up in hell, which here means more than the grave but the abode of the wicked dead. Lazarus, the poor beggar, ends up on another realm where the rich man could see Lazarus by the side of Abraham. Should we believe literally that those who are in hell can look up and see the righteous with Abraham? Indeed, the formerly rich man can actually speak to Abraham. He begs Abraham to send Lazarus to dip his finger in water to cool his tongue as he is in agony in the fire.

Abraham replies that there is a gulf that cannot be crossed. Therefore the request cannot be fulfilled. In addition, his suffering is the justice of God due to his behavior on earth.

The former rich man begs Abraham to send Lazarus to warn his brothers so that they do not come to the place of suffering. Abraham responds that if they do not hear Moses and the prophets, they will not respond even if someone from the dead goes to them. The teaching of Abraham and the prophets is sufficient for turning to God and being saved.

In this account the judgment is experienced after death, before the resurrection. Hell anticipates Gehenna, the lake of fire. The realm of comfort and blessing attained by Lazarus anticipates the good end in the age to come. We cannot take this passage to indicate final destinies, since Yeshua was clear throughout His teaching on the future resurrection. Rather, it may be an indication of the intermediate state, between death and the resurrection. Yet, since we do not know with clarity the literal and the figurative dimensions of this story, we should not press the details. This passage is helpful in debunking theories like that of the Seventh Day Adventists that states that when a person dies he ceases to be and in the resurrection he is re-created.

In Luke 18:18, the rich ruler asks Yeshua what he must do to inherit eternal life. Yeshua begins with the commandments. Yeshua did not repeat them all, and it is of special note that He did not include the command to not covet (v. 20). Yeshua, as in the Sermon on the Mount, deals with the commands by going to the desires of the heart. So Yeshua tests him on the issue of coveting and says, "Sell everything you have and give to the poor, and you will have treasure in heaven. Then come and follow me" (v. 22). When he heard this he became sad because he had great wealth (v. 23). As in Matthew, Yeshua says, "How hard it is for the rich to enter the kingdom of God.

Indeed, it is easier for a camel to go through the eye of a needle than for a rich man to enter the kingdom of God" (v. 25).

The Kingdom of God is a present reality to be entered. One lives in and from the Kingdom and its provisions (Matt. 6:33–34). The Kingdom also includes the final good destiny of the righteous. Considering wealth as a sign of God's favor, the disciples ask who then can be saved (Luke 18:26). Yeshua responds that though it is not possible for man on his own, "What is impossible with man is possible with God" (v. 27). Indeed, there were rich men that responded to Yeshua and followed Him. Those who follow Him, and leave all to do so, are assured of provision in this age and in the age to come, everlasting life (vv. 29–30).

Is the rich ruler who could not respond to Yeshua's challenge eternally lost? The text does not say, but a righteous life and attaining eternal life requires that the deepest motives of the heart are God-motives and not self motives including all kinds of idolatry, such as putting self before God.

In Luke 19:1–9 we read the story of Zacchaeus, a tax collector. He wanted to see Yeshua as He was passing through Jericho. He ran ahead and climbed a sycamore fig tree to see Him. When Yeshua saw him, He spoke prophetically, "Zacchaeus, come down immediately. I must stay at your house today" (v. 5).

Something about Yeshua greatly affected Zacchaeus. He responds, "Look, Lord! Here and now I give half of my possessions to the poor, and if I have cheated anybody out of anything [quite usual among tax collectors], I will pay back four times the amount" (v. 8).

Yeshua responds in verse 9–10:

> Today salvation has come to this house, because this
> man, too, is a son of Abraham. For the Son of Man
> came to seek and save what was lost.

Yeshua proclaims his salvation, which includes entering
into the realm of salvation in the immediate and a state
of everlasting life in the age to come. Two things are
evident in the account. One is that Zacchaeus believes in
Yeshua. How much about Him did he believe? He did not
know of His death for our sins. In addition, he showed
true repentance by giving half of his wealth and paying
restitution. It is interesting, in the light of the earlier story
of the rich young ruler, that Yeshua does not challenge
him to give away all his wealth. Apparently giving away
half showed his true heart.

In the Luke account of the Crucifixion, one the
criminals being crucified next to Yeshua mocks him,
whereas the other believes in Him. He requests that Yeshua
remember him when He comes into His Kingdom. Yeshua
responds, "Today you will be with me in paradise" (23:43).
This coheres with the text in Luke 16 where Lazarus is in
a good place before the resurrection. Here Yeshua asserts
not the end of the person at death but continuation in a
place called paradise. Apparently this is the state of the
person until the resurrection from the dead.

Finally Luke ends with the resurrected Messiah
proclaiming:

> This is what is written: The Christ will suffer and
> rise from the dead on the third day, and repentance
> and forgiveness of sins will be preached in his name
> to all nations, beginning at Jerusalem.
>
> —LUKE 24:46–47

This certainly implies that those who embrace repentance and forgiveness in Yeshua will have a good final end destiny, both in the state after death and in the resurrection from the dead. Other texts add that one must continue in the way thus chosen.

Summary of the Synoptic Gospels (Matthew, Mark, and Luke)

As noted, we used Matthew for the texts that are paralleled in Mark and Luke. These Gospels present a large amount of material on the afterlife. Generally the teaching of Yeshua states that there will be a future judgment at the end of this age. In that judgment, the righteous will enter into a state of blessing and joy. The wicked will enter into a realm of terrible suffering, which is commonly described in terms of "weeping and the gnashing of teeth." The judgment is truly terrible, to be greatly feared, and to be avoided at all costs. Those who are judged righteous will enter into a life of joy, a bodily life or resurrection life where they will be like the angels of God. They will not have sexual relations (they neither marry nor are given in marriage). The age to come for the righteous is described as a great banquet, a wedding feast, and a time of great rewards according to good works. It is important to note that the age to come is a real physical age with real physical bodies that transcend the limits of our present physical bodies. C. S. Lewis was brilliant in his descriptions in *Mere Christianity*[1] as is N. T. Wright in his *Surprised by Hope*.[2]

The texts of these three Gospels generally speak of the destiny of the wicked as a time of continued pain and loss. Everlasting punishment is a reasonable inference from these texts. However, there are other texts that seem to say that the wicked will ultimately become extinct. Scholars have wrestled with these two possibilities. C. S. Lewis tried to solve it by the idea that the wicked suffer after death but have a kind of half-life where there are ceasing to be forever, like the half-life of radioactive material. The more grossly wicked will suffer more. The immediate cessation of life for the wicked would not seem to be fair since some are so much more wicked than others.[3] The Synoptic Gospels speak consistently of a final and great separation of the wicked and the righteous.

The punishment is described as eternal. Does this mean that it is never reversed and that the lost are truly and forever lost? It would seem to be the case. What about people who are between wicked and righteous? Could there be a purgatory for those who are neither greatly wicked nor righteous? There are no texts that speak of this in the Synoptic Gospels.

So this raises the larger question. Who is in the category of the righteous and who is in the category of the wicked? There are several texts that give a variety of answers. We do not find totally clear answers to all our questions about final destinies in the Synoptic Gospels. However, we do find a sufficient teaching content for our basic conclusions on the issues. There is the category of the righteous of whom it is said they will not lose their reward. Those who respond to the message of the good news of the Kingdom and repent and follow Yeshua are in the category of the righteous. They enter the Kingdom and have a wonderful eternal destiny. Indeed, this is the most important category of those who are accepted as righteous even if their life, before this decision, was wicked. Note especially the thief on the cross. However, those who give a cup of water to a young disciple, because he is a disciple, will not lose their reward. Also those who live in loyalty to God and to fulfill His will are also spoken of as fitting the category of the righteous. However, this is not righteousness by works since such people know their own sin and depend on the mercy and forgiveness of God. The beggar Lazarus fits this description.

Who is in the wicked category? Religious hypocrites are the number one category of the wicked in the teaching of Yeshua. This is because religious hypocrites turn people away from God, or at least God as He should be known and understood. The hypocrite makes his convert twice the child of hell. Hypocrites persecute the truly righteous. Religious hypocrites are not watching for the Kingdom and the coming of Yeshua. As the wicked head steward beats the servants of his master and abuses others through his position, so the wicked act in parallel ways. In addition, those who live primarily for self and not for others and are not living motivated by love are in the category of the wicked. Also among the wicked is the man who built his storage barns and did not consider the needs of others but only his own ease of life. The rich man goes to the suffering realm of Hades since he did not show mercy to the poor (Lazarus) and lived a life of selfish luxury. However, the most important category of the wicked lost are those who reject the convicting work of the Spirit in the context of Yeshua's great works. These blaspheme the Spirit, and for this there is no forgiveness forever.

REBECCA SPRINGER

Rebecca Springer, at a time of weakness and near death, is taken on a journey to heaven (or a vision of the age to come) guided by her brother-in-law:

He led me through a doorway, between marble columns, into a large reception hall whose inlaid floor, mullioned window, and broad, low stairway captivated me at once....Turning to the left, he led me through the beautiful marble columns that substituted for doorways into a large, oblong room....The entire walls and floor of the room were still made of that exquisite light gray marble, polished to the greatest luster. But over the walls and floors were strewn gorgeous, long-stemmed roses, of every variety and color, from the deepest crimson to the most delicate shades of pink and yellow.[4]

In another room she describes

a semicircular row of shelves, supported by very delicate pillars of gray marble, about six feet high, extended some fifteen feet into the spacious main room and cut it into two sections lengthwise...."Why do they have books in heaven?" I asked. "Why not?" What strange ideas we mortals have of the pleasures and duties of this blessed life! We seem to think that the death of the body means an entire change to the soul. But that is not the case by any means. We bring to this life the same tastes, the same desires and the same knowledge we had before death. If these were not sufficiently pure and good to form a part of this life, then we ourselves may not enter. What would be the use of our long lives, given to the pursuit of certain worth and legitimate knowledge, if at death it all counts as nothing, and we begin this life on a wholly different line of thought and study.[5]

On a trip to and descent into a heavenly lake we read as follows:

I lay watching this marvelous panorama (the colors deepened and faded like the lights of the aurora borealis)....The waters of this lake catch the light in a most marvelous manner.[6]

In a journey to the temple we read:

A long flight of low, broad steps in gradations rose from where we stood to the door of the Temple. They, too, were of solid pearl bordered on either side by channels paved with golden stones through which flowed crystal waters that met and mingled in one stream far out upon the plain....The immense dome, at that moment filled with a luminous cloud, was upheld by three rows of massive pillars of gold. The walls and floors were made of pearl, as was the great platform that took up at least one third of the Temple on the eastern side. There were no seats of any kind. The great golden pillars stood like rows of sentinels on the shining floor. A railing of gold ran entirely around the platform on three sides, so that it was inaccessible from the body of the Temple. Beneath this railing, on the Temple floor, a pearl kneeling-step encircled the platform, also made of pearl. In the center of the platform an immense altar of gold arose. It was supported by seraphs of gold with outspread wings, one at each corner....Suddenly, we saw the draperies tremble and glow until a radiance far beyond the splendor of the sun at midday shone through them. The whole Temple was "filled with the glory of the LORD" (Exodus 40:34). We saw, in the midst of the luminous cloud that filled the dome, the forms of angelic harpers. As we dropped with bowed heads beside the altar-rail and hid our faces from the "brightness of His coming" we heard the

trumpet-call of the four angels around the altar. The
voices of celestial harpers sang:

Holy, Holy, Holy, LORD God Almighty.
All Thy works shall praise Thy name,
In earth, and sky and sea.
Holy, Holy, Holy, merciful and mighty,
God in three persons—blessed Trinity. Amen.[7, 8]

Chapter 6

THE GOSPEL OF JOHN

THE EMPHASIS OF the first three Gospels is on the person of Yeshua and His proclamation of the Kingdom of God. The Kingdom has come in His person and ministry, and people are invited to enter into that realm by repenting and embracing the good news and following Yeshua. This assures their good eternal destiny. The idea of entering the Kingdom and having an everlasting good destiny is clearly found in John 3. One enters the Kingdom of God in the immediate response to the gospel, but this Kingdom life is forever. However, after John 3, the concept of the Kingdom of God is presented mostly under the term "eternal life." This is John's parallel phrase for the Kingdom of God.

Our study begins with the familiar text in John 3. Yeshua says to Nicodemus that "no one can see the kingdom of God unless he is born again" (v. 3). In response to Nicodemus's puzzlement, Yeshua says that one must be born of water and the Spirit (v. 5). Traditional historic church Christians see "born of water" as speaking of baptism. More recent evangelicals see this speaking of a totally supernatural and spiritual transaction, an operation on the heart, the inner man. The context is Ezekiel 36, which is speaking of the new covenant though it does not use the term. It is quite parallel to Jeremiah 31:31. This born-again experience is like the wind. One can see the effects of the wind, but the wind itself is unseen. So there is an unseen work of the Spirit that produces a heart change. Responding rightly to Yeshua effects this heart change.

The text says nothing about the good final destiny or bad final destiny of those who came before the time of Yeshua. It does not speak about those who have not yet had an opportunity to respond to Yeshua; though John 1:9 tells us that wisdom, or logos, was the light for all. It implies that this light could be received. But John tells us as well in the same chapter that most did not respond, so God sent His Son to bring the maximum potential of positive responses. While we may speculate about those who have not yet had the opportunity to hear the gospel, once it is heard in the power and presence of the Spirit, a decision must be made; and that decision seals one's eternal destiny. So a new era is starting where the response to Yeshua is the key to a person's eternal destiny. John is an existential Gospel. God gave His Son that human beings might have everlasting life! Yeshua came that "everyone who believes in him may have eternal life" (John 3:15). Then, of course, we read the most familiar verse that "God so loved the world that he gave his one and only Son, that whoever believes in him shall not perish but have eternal life" (v. 16). Again, for John, everlasting life or eternal life begins when the response is positive.

The response to the Son brings a division between those who have eternal life and those who experience God's wrath: "Whoever believes in the Son has eternal life, but whoever rejects the Son will not see life, for God's wrath remains on him" (v. 36).

The verse does not clearly speak of the separation of the righteous and the wicked at the final judgment like the first three Gospels and other texts in John. It rather speaks of the ongoing state of the wicked, those who reject the Son, to not see life but to experience God's wrath. Can the person still turn back after their rejection and change their mind and life direction? The text does not say, but continuing in a stance of rejection perpetuates the state of wrath; and as we will see in John, it can also be eternal.

In John 5:28–29 we read of an ultimate separation in a final judgment. The Son is given authority to judge. He will call forth the dead.

> Do not be amazed at this, for a time is coming when all who are in their graves will hear his voice and come out—those who have done what is good will rise to live, and those who have done what is evil will rise to be condemned.

The language of the text is interesting. The state of those who have done good is simply described as rising to live, but evildoers are condemned. What does their state in condemnation look like? How long does it last? John often leaves an element of mystery. The text is quite close to the parallel in Daniel 12.

The concept of eternal life is again presented in John 6:27:

> Do not work for food that spoils, but for food that endures to eternal life, which the Son of Man will give you.

The idea here is that people change through the Word of the Son, and what that food produces will last. It produces the quality of life that is eternal. Again in John 6:39–40:

> And this is the will of him who sent me, that I shall
> lose none of all those he has given me, but raise
> them up at the last day. For my Father's will is that
> everyone who looks to the Son and believes in him
> shall have eternal life, and I will raise them up at
> the last day

This raising on the last day is again repeated in verse 44.

We note here that looking to the Son, believing in Him, results in eternal life. The implication is that it produces the kind of change such that the person will be in the category of those who do good (5:29).

The person who eats of the bread from heaven, the living bread, Yeshua, will live forever (3:51). The text then goes on to speak about eating His flesh, which traditional church doctrine understands as connected to Communion (the Eucharist, or the Lord's Supper). This is part of the life of His followers. But while Communion is a participation in His life, believing and receiving His Word is also life giving.

> Whoever eats my flesh and drinks my blood remains
> in me, and I in them. . . . the one who feeds on me
> will live because of me. . . . He who feeds on this
> bread will live forever.
>
> —John 6:56–58

Eternal life or everlasting life is again promised to Yeshua's disciples in John 10:27–30:

> My sheep listen to my voice; I know them, and
> they follow me. I give them eternal life, and they
> shall never perish; no one can snatch them out of
> my hand. My Father, who has given them to me, is

greater than all; no one can snatch them out of my Father's hand. I and the Father are one.

A good everlasting destiny is promised but there is also assurance of God's keeping power.

John 11:21–26 is a very important passage, one frequently memorized. The context is Yeshua's raising Lazarus from the dead. The dialogue is with Martha. The body of her brother was in his tomb.

> "Lord," Martha said to Jesus, "if you had been here, my brother would not have died. But I know that even now God will give you whatever you ask." Jesus said to her, "Your brother will rise again." Martha answered, "I know he will rise again in the resurrection at the last day." Jesus said to her, "I am the resurrection and the life. The one who believes in me will live, even though they die; and whoever lives by believing in me will never die. Do you believe this?'"

There is no description of what this everlasting state will look like, but it is obviously wonderful.

A wonderfully comforting passage about everlasting life is found in John 14:1–3:

> Do not let your hearts be troubled. You believe in God believe also in me. My Father's house has many rooms; if that were not so, would I have told you that I am going there to prepare a place for you? And if I go and prepare a place for you, I will come back and take you to be with me that you also may be where I am.

This text leaves us with questions. Where is that room being prepared? Doesn't the Bible teach that our destiny is with Him on a renewed earth? This is brilliantly argued by Bishop N. T. Wright in his book *Surprised by Hope*.[1] So is Yeshua preparing something in heaven that will be manifest on earth? Or, is He preparing a place of dwelling for us in the time between our death and the resurrection of the dead? When He says that He will come back and take us to be with Him, is this at our death where He will meet us or is He speaking of His second coming at the end of this age? None of these questions are resolved in this text. We do have teaching on an intermediate state before the resurrection in Paul and the Book of Revelation. These texts will be reviewed. Nothing in this text contradicts the clarification of the later texts, but this text is both comforting and mysterious.

The mystery continues in John 17:24, a part of a section where Yeshua prays intensely for the unity of His followers:

> Father, I want those you have given me to be with me where I am, and to see my glory, the glory you have given me because you loved me before the creation of the world.

In this passage, I would conclude that He is speaking of a connection to heaven where His glory is revealed. In Ephesians 2 we read that we are already spiritually connected to Him and said to be seated with Him now in heavenly places (v. 6). So was Yeshua praying for this experience of our perceiving this place we now have with Him, or to be with Him in heaven in the intermediate state, or to be with Him in His glory in His second coming? Is John recording a prayer for the Second Coming? When we are in proper unity, the Lord will return. All of these options are possible and none are precluded. John often speaks with double meanings, and all these meanings can be intended. The mysterious way of speaking is meant to be unpacked with deeper meanings.

CONCLUSIONS ON THE GOSPEL OF JOHN

For John, eternal life begins when one responds rightly to Yeshua. This leads to an everlasting and wonderful final destiny. When one is rightly related to Yeshua, he or she has assurance of that destiny. Believing in Him is a trusting relationship that changes the person to one who walks in the light. However, John does open a door to the possibility that that one can be related to Yeshua without responding to the historical information about the historical Yeshua. This is because He is the light that lights every man that comes into the world (John 1:9). Yeshua was the revealer, the Word before His incarnation. He may still be a revealer that transcends historical knowledge about Him. However, this possibility of response, noted by John Wesley,[2] is not emphasized. Rather the emphasis in John was in response to the incarnated Yeshua and believing in Him during His lifetime and also to respond to the message about Yeshua after His resurrection and ascension. The Holy Spirit brings conviction so that one can respond to this information. The emphasis is on hearing the gospel so that one might be saved, or have assurance of eternal life.

RICK JOYNER

Many consider Rick Joyner a prophet. This excerpt is from his amazing book *The Final Quest* and gives a visionary picture of the age to come.

The path soon opened into a hall so large that I did not think the earth itself could contain it. Its beauty could not even be described by any reference to the human architecture. This exceeded the wonder of anything I had yet experienced, including the Garden and the chamber that held the treasures of salvation. By now I was as overwhelmed with joy and beauty as I had been overwhelmed by darkness and fear just minutes before....At the far end was the Source of the glory that was emanating from everything else in the room. I knew that it was the Lord Himself, and though I had now seen Him many times, I began to be a bit afraid as I walked toward Him. However, this fear was a holy fear that only magnified the great joy and peace that I also felt. Not only was the judgment seat of Christ a source of more security than I had ever experienced, but at the same time it was the source of a greater and purer fear. I did not notice how great the distance was to the throne. It was so wonderful just to walk here that I did not care if it took me a thousand years to get there. In earthly terms, it did take me a very long time. In one sense I felt that it was days, and in another, years. But somehow earthly time had no relevance here. I noticed that I was passing multitudes of people who were standing in ranks to my left (there was just as many to my right, but they were so far away that I could not see them until I reached the throne. As I looked at them, I had to stop. They were dazzling, more regal than anyone I had ever seen. Their countenances were captivating).[3]

Chapter 7

THE BOOK OF ACTS

THE MESSAGE PETER brings in Acts 2 on the Day of Pentecost is the first post-Resurrection apostolic proclamation of the gospel. In this text, responding rightly to the message of the gospel is the way to a wonderful and everlasting life. Acts 2:21 quotes from Joel 2:32: "Everyone who calls on the name of the LORD will be saved." The crowd at Pentecost is told to

> repent and be baptized, every one of you, in the name of Jesus Christ for the forgiveness of your sins. And you will receive the gift of the Holy Spirit.
>
> —ACTS 2:38

In addition, he said, "Save yourselves from this corrupt generation" (v. 40).

We should note that a Jewish view at that time was the concept of salvation as the corporate salvation of the nation, so we should not read all texts as merely about individual destinies. I think it is a good inference that this text is looking toward an individual's final destiny and avoiding the ultimate judgment of God.

Peter also presents Yeshua as remaining in heaven "until the time comes for God to restore everything, as he promised long ago through his holy prophets" (3:21). The picture of the restoration of all things is a picture of a fully restored earth and of the participation of the righteous of the ages through the resurrection from the dead.

Acts 4:12 is an often quoted verse:

> Salvation is found in no one else, for there is no other name under heaven given to mankind by which we must be saved.

It is too easy to read a later more evangelical individualism into this passage and think of it as speaking about the individual gaining a good place in heaven. But for a first century Jewish person, salvation includes the destiny of the individual but also the deliverance of Israel from her enemies and entering into her promised national destiny. There is no other name whereby the salvation of Israel as a nation will be affected. We see this corporate aspect in the prayers that surrounded the conceptions and births of John the Baptist and Yeshua: "He has raised up a horn of salvation for us... salvation from our enemies and from the hand of all who hate us" (Luke 1:69, 71).

The preaching in the Book of Acts does not *always* explicitly emphasize the everlasting good destiny of the individual who submits to the gospel and embraces Yeshua as Lord. However, as in the preaching of Peter in the house of Cornelius (10:43), the promise of forgiveness of sins through believing in Yeshua in the first century context would include the idea of a good everlasting destiny after this life.

We note the same emphasis on the forgiveness of sins at Pisidian Antioch and being justified (or being made or declared righteous before God) (13:38–39). It seems that the Book of Acts is still emphasizing that the embrace of Yeshua by Jews and Gentiles moves history toward the great climax of the return of Yeshua and the redemption of the world. In Acts 13:46 Paul declares that those who rejected the message "do not consider yourselves worthy of eternal life." But again there is no description of what that life looks like or will look like.

In Acts 15 we read about the controversy over Gentiles being required to be circumcised and to keep the whole Law of Moses. The circumcision party held the view that without this one could not be saved (v. 1). Again, in this context, being saved includes participation in the glories of the age to come. This participation is promised to the faithful who have died. The debate in Acts 15 is over who is included as within this fold, and by implication, assured of their eternal life. The conclusion of the apostles and elders is voiced by Jacob (James) that the people coming to God through the gospel are the fulfillment of Amos 9:11–12 (Acts 15:16–17). It states that the rebuilding of David's tent will be the occasion of the remnant of men from the nations coming to David's restored tabernacle. These who bear His name will seek the Lord. This is really only the beginning of the fulfillment that will be completed when Yeshua returns. The Gentiles are thus released from the requirement of Jewish life.

The story of the incarceration of Paul and Silas is recounted in Acts 16. As they worshipped, an earthquake opened the prison cells. The terrified jailor "called for lights, rushed in and fell trembling before Paul and Silas. He then brought them out and asked, 'Sirs, what must I do to be saved?'" (vv. 29–30).

They answered, "Believe in the Lord Jesus, and you will be saved—you and your household" (v. 31). The word *saved* includes a destiny of blessing after death, a destiny of blessing in the age to come, but also a life of present provision and purpose. However, in the context of the ancient world, the jailor perceived God's supernatural intervention and probably sought to both avoid immediate judgment and to attain an ultimately good destiny after death. He would not have had a concept of the age to come on earth.

Paul's speech to the Athenians on the Areopagus (17:19–34) presented Jesus as the future judge of the world. The proof of this was the Resurrection. The judgment Paul had in mind was after death or at the return of Yeshua as we know from other Pauline texts, but the limited content of these statements does not give us any great detail on this matter.

Paul responds to his accusers after his arrest in Jerusalem saying, "My brothers, I am a Pharisee, the son of a Pharisee. I stand on trial because of my hope in the resurrection of the dead" (23:6). This led to a great dispute between the Pharisees and the Sadducees. Paul's statement was readily understood in the context of the teaching of the Pharisees that the righteous of the Jewish people would attain a positive final destiny in the age to come through the resurrection of the dead. Judaism later applied this positive final destiny to the righteous of all nations, which included forsaking idols, embracing the one and only true God, and following His basic moral laws.

Paul's identification with the Pharisees on this doctrine is repeated in Acts 24:15. However, he adds the important point that the resurrection includes the righteous and the wicked with the implication that the wicked will be judged in bodily form. There is thus an afterlife for the wicked, at least for a time.

Paul grounds the resurrection of Yeshua on the very fact that the Pharisees and Jewish people largely believed in a future resurrection, so it should not be thought incredible that He was raised from the dead. In Paul's defense before King Agrippa, he quotes what Yeshua said to him, giving information not found in earlier accounts. In Acts 26:6–8 he asserts:

> And now it is because of my hope in what God has promised our ancestors that I am on trial today. This is the promise our twelve tribes are hoping to see fulfilled as they earnestly serve God day and night. King Agrippa, it is because of this hope that these Jews are accusing me. Why should any of you consider it incredible that God raises the dead?

Of course, it was not the common Jewish hope that the Messiah would die and be raised from the dead, but Paul defends the resurrection of Yeshua in the light of the hope of the resurrection from the dead that was part of the first century Jewish faith of many.

In verses 17 and 18, with regard to being sent to the Gentiles, Yeshua said to Paul:

> I am sending you to them to open their eyes and turn them from darkness to light, and from the power of Satan to God, so that they may receive forgiveness of sins and a place among those who are sanctified by faith in me.

We see more than a hint that this place among those sanctified is a place with the Jewish righteous and envisions a positive destiny in the age to come. It is by turning from Satan to God, through repentance, that they will receive forgiveness. This implies embracing Yeshua as Lord. Paul continues in verse 20: "I preached that they should repent and turn to God and demonstrate their repentance by their deeds."

HOWARD STROM

Howard Strom describes a death experience where he descended into hell. After it, he dedicated his life to Jesus. He eventually became a United Church of Christ (Congregationalist) minister. He describes the experience of going to hell and also painted pictures of his experience. This is one of the most amazing descriptions of a death experience and descent into hell of which I am aware.

He describes his descent into hell as being under the power of evil human beings who have died.

> While I couldn't see in this total darkness, every sound and every physical sensation registered with horrifying intensity. These creatures were once human beings. The best way I can describe them is to think of the worst imaginable person stripped of every impulse of compassion. Some of them seemed to be able to tell others what to do, but I had no sense of there being any organization to the mayhem. They didn't appear to be controlled or directed by anyone. Simply, they were a mob of beings totally driven by unbridled cruelty. In that darkness I had intense physical contact with them when they swarmed over me. Their bodies felt exactly as human bodies do except for two characteristics. They had very long, sharp fingernails, and their teeth were longer than normal. I'd never been bitten by a human being before this....The level of noise was excruciating. Countless people laughed, yelled, and jeered. In the middle of this bedlam I was the object of their desire. My torment was their excitement.[1]

Chapter 8

THE PAULINE EPISTLES

THE BOOK OF ROMANS

The argument of Romans 1 and 2 concerning the corruption and sin of the human race presupposes a judgment after death. This is also true of the whole Book of Romans and is implicitly and explicitly found throughout the book. The idea is found in Romans 2:3 where Paul asks, "Do you think you will escape God's judgment?" And then in verse 4 he says, "God's kindness leads you toward repentance." So also in verses 6 through 11 we read:

> God "will repay each person according to what they have done." To those who by persistence in doing good seek glory, honor and immortality, he will give eternal life. 8 But for those who are self-seeking and who reject the truth and follow evil, there will be wrath and anger. There will be trouble and distress for every human being who does evil: first for the Jew, then for the Gentile; but glory, honor and peace for everyone who does good: first for the Jew, then for the Gentile. For God does not show favoritism.

The passage is quite noteworthy since it seems to be teaching that the ultimate judgment will be not merely according to who has and who has not embraced Yeshua, but is determined by one's response to life itself where one chooses goodness and righteousness and not self-seeking and evil. This gives credibility to those who argue that there are people who are included in the salvation of Yeshua who have not explicitly embraced Him. On the other hand, those who do not embrace a wider hope view would say that only those who have explicitly embraced Jesus can seek for glory, honor, and righteousness. The text does not explicitly say this. Indeed, the passage seems to explicitly refer to people who are not in the stream of biblical revelation in verses 14–16 where Paul states:

> (Indeed, when Gentiles, who do not have the law, do by nature things required by the law, they are a law for themselves, even though they do not have the law. They show that the requirements of the law are written on their hearts, their consciences also bearing witness, and their thoughts sometimes accusing them and at other times even defending them.) This will take place on the day when God judges people's secrets through Jesus Christ, as my gospel declares.

Paul thus opens the possibility of the one not circumcised who obeys the law as condemning those who have been circumcised but are lawbreakers. The text does not say that those doing the condemning have explicitly embraced Yeshua.

These texts as well as John 1 were the basis of John Wesley's view that people could respond to God and be moving toward a positive final destiny, though they had not explicitly responded to the gospel.[1] Even so, for Wesley this was an exceptional category, as shown by Romans 1 and its description of the human race. Yet Romans 3 makes it quite clear that it is only by the grace of God and the sacrifice of Yeshua that people are saved, for no one will be declared righteous by observing the law. This does not preclude a right response for some who have not heard the gospel and thereby to be in a state that Wesley called prevenient grace.[2]

The argument of Romans 5 is that death came to the human race through one man's sin, Adam; so life comes through one man's obedience, and this is not only to reign in this life (vv. 16–17). It is the reversal of the sentence of death through the Resurrection, as will be asserted in other Pauline texts. We should note that some universalists (who believe all human beings will eventually be saved) use Romans 5:18–19 as a proof text. It says:

> Consequently, just as one trespass resulted in condemnation for all people, so also one righteous act resulted in justification and life for all people. For just as through the disobedience of the one man the many were made sinners, so also through the obedience of the one man the many will be made righteous.

The use of this text to prove universalism seems a bit stretched since there are so many other texts that would lead us to believe that the justification is potentially there for all who receive it but not automatically there for everyone. In the same way, universalists use Romans 11:32: "For God has bound all men over to disobedience so that he may have mercy on them all."

Whether this is a universal offer or a universal certainty of salvation for all would seem to be according to the qualification of other Pauline texts. There are so many other texts that we will interpret that speak of an ultimate judgment of those who continued in sin, where one will not enter the Kingdom of God either in this life or in the age to come.

Romans 6 speaks of the co-death and resurrection

experienced by the followers of Yeshua. The result of this co-death and resurrection is eternal life: "For the wages of sin is death, but the gift of God is eternal life in Christ Jesus our Lord" (v. 23). The definite promise of a wonderful afterlife is assured to those who are in Yeshua.

Romans 8 teaches that the Spirit of God that raised Yeshua from the dead will give life to our mortal bodies (v. 11). This may mean the energizing of our bodies in this life and not the future resurrection. Those who are alive at His second coming may experience that translation where life is given to their mortal bodies so that they become immortal. It is not certain what the verse is indicating. However, the rest of Romans 8 teaches that there will be a revealed glory that makes our present sufferings not worth comparing (v. 18). This glory is described as the revelation of the sons of God (vv. 14–17). The whole creation waits for this (v. 19). This is the goal of this age. The language speaks of the children of God being brought into their state of resurrection or translated glory (v. 21). So also, we groan in the Spirit as we wait for our adoption; that is the redemption of our bodies (v. 23). Paul says that it is in this hope we were saved; and because of this hope of ultimate resurrection or the translation of our bodies at His coming, we know that nothing can separate us from the love of God, including death (vv. 25–38).

In Romans 10:9–10 we read the classic verse:

> If you declare with your mouth, "Jesus is Lord," and believe in your heart that God raised him from the dead, you will be saved. For it is with your heart that you believe and are justified, and it is with your mouth that you profess your faith and are saved.

Then in Romans 10:13 we read, "Everyone who calls on the Lord will be saved."

Many have stressed that this salvation includes the experience of new life at this present time. Yet salvation includes that extremely important matter of our destiny after death. This gives us very important biblical information as to who is definitely included in this positive destiny after death. It is those who confess Yeshua as Lord and believe in Him in their hearts. This does imply embracing a life of obedience to Him as our Lord.

In Romans 11 we read the amazing account of the partial hardening of the nation of Israel, but then her ultimate salvation. The text affirms that ultimately "all Israel will be saved." This salvation is a national deliverance, but in keeping with the Pharisaic understanding of the first century, it includes the resurrection and everlasting life.

In Romans 13:11 we read that "our salvation is nearer now than when we first believed." This salvation is looking toward the Second Coming, the resurrection, and our being transformed into His likeness.

1 AND 2 CORINTHIANS

As in Romans and the other Pauline letters, the word *salvation* includes an everlasting life beyond death in glorified bodies. I therefore will not note every use of the word. First Corinthians, however, adds content to the glorious hope of what awaits us in the life beyond this one.

First Corinthians 2:9–10 states:

> "What no eye has seen, what no ear has heard, and what no human mind has conceived"—the things God has prepared for those who love him—these are the things God has revealed to us by his Spirit.

Yet what God has revealed is partial. The glorious life of the age to come is beyond what we can fully conceive.

In 1 Corinthians 3:10–15 Paul warns that those who seek to build in the context of congregational life can build what will not last but will be like wood, hay, and straw. He refers to "the Day" (v. 13), which is the Day of Judgment. Fire will test the quality of each man's work. If what he built survives the fire of judgment, he will receive a reward. The nature of this reward is not here specified. However, if the works do not survive the judgment, the person can be saved, but as one escaping through flames. This text is not speaking of the judgment of the wicked, but of those who are not building in the Kingdom of God with quality.

Chapter 4 verse 5 notes that God will bring to light the motives of men's hearts, and that at that time, each will "receive his praise from God."

There are clearly differences in reward that are based on how we live and how we build, but within the boundaries of a basic righteousness as we read in 1 Corinthians 6:9–11.

> Or do you not know that wrongdoers will not inherit the kingdom of God? Do not be deceived: Neither the sexually immoral nor idolaters nor adulterers nor men who have sex with men nor thieves nor the greedy nor drunkards nor slanderers nor swindlers will inherit the kingdom of God. And that is what some of you were. But you were washed, you were sanctified....

It is important to note that there are behavioral boundaries that mark the saved from the lost. The inheritance of the Kingdom of God begins now, but here

Paul envisions the future everlasting inheritance and the exclusion of those who lead a wicked life.

Again with regard to rewards, Paul presents this life as a race where we compete to gain a crown. The crown is available to all who run faithfully with a disciplined, fruitful life (9:24–27). The nature of rewards is again not yet clarified.

In chapter 15 we find the most important passage in the Bible about the nature of the resurrection body with regard to those who have died or the transformed body of those who are alive at His coming. The certainty of our resurrection is based on His resurrection. Life in the age to come for those who are saved is a life in glorified bodies that are not subject to sickness and many of the limitations that we know in this life. Paul's teaching strains the limits of human language distinctions to describe the new bodies that will be ours. The body that dies is like a seed (vv. 35–38). This should alert us to the foolishness of the practices that seek to preserve the body and to keep it from going back to earth. In the Orthodox Jewish view, the allowance of the body's return to the earth is embraced. Just as a plant dies, it is not the whole plant that matters but the seed. This is quite interesting in the light of DNA. There will be a connection between the resurrection body and our earthly body. Yet the body that is raised is imperishable, glorious, powerful, and is a spiritual body (v. 48). The idea of a spiritual body seems almost incoherent; but if we probe more deeply, it is a physical body that is so permeated by the Spirit and our renewal power that it does not have the physical limits of this world, so it is called a spiritual body (vv. 42–48). This is described as the likeness of Jesus, the Man from heaven (v. 49).

Flesh and blood as we know it in this life cannot inherit

the Kingdom of God (v. 50). The resurrection body is not flesh and blood as we understand it. The perishable does not inherit the imperishable (v. 51).

This will apply not only to those whose bodies have been sown into the earth. Rather, those who are alive at His coming will be changed, "in a flash, in the twinkling of an eye, at the last trumpet" (v. 51). The glorious words on the resurrection and change of those who are alive at His coming bear repeating:

> The trumpet will sound, the dead will be raised imperishable, and we will be changed. For the perishable must clothe itself with the imperishable, and the mortal with immortality. When the perishable has been clothed with the imperishable, and the mortal with immortality, then the saying that is written will come true: "Death has been swallowed up in victory."
>
> —1 CORINTHIANS 15:52–54

Thus it can be said, "Death has been swallowed up in victory" (v. 54). This is the most ringing affirmation that the life of the saved in the age to come is a glorified physical life. It is more analogous to our life in the present though vastly different. It is so much more attractive than the idea of a disembodied soul that simply floats somewhere in the beyond.

One verse in this chapter favored by universalists is 1 Corinthians 15:22: "For as in Adam all die, so in Christ all will be made alive." The universalists want to hold from this verse that all will be eventually saved; whereas the non-universalists qualify it with the many other verses on judgment and hold that it is only about all who will be made alive or who have put their trust in Yeshua.

It says in 2 Corinthians 1:22-23 that "he anointed us, set his seal of ownership on us, and put his Spirit in our hearts as a deposit, guaranteeing what is to come."

Here the Holy Spirit is the guarantee of our destiny in the age to come. The ministry of the new covenant brings righteousness, life, and glory that lasts (2 Cor. 3:10). As ministers, they spread the fragrance of the knowledge of Messiah. It is the aroma of Messiah among those being saved (2:16). Being saved again includes the destiny of a wonderful everlasting life. However, for to those who are perishing (probably those who reject the gospel), it is the smell of death that entails the loss of such a positive destiny. Again, in 2 Corinthians 4, the gospel is veiled from those who are perishing and do not see the glory of Messiah (v. 3). The idea of perishing could be taken to imply that they are headed toward ceasing to be as their ultimate end. However, I do not think we should over press this language.

Of those who have embraced the good news, Paul states, "We know that the one who raised the Lord Jesus from the dead will also raise us with Jesus and present us with you in his presence" (v. 14).

Second Corinthians 5 includes an exceedingly important passage on the destiny of the believer in Yeshua after death:

> For we know that if the earthly tent we live in is destroyed, we have a building from God, an eternal house in heaven, not built by human hands. Meanwhile we groan, longing to be clothed instead with our heavenly dwelling . . . so that what is mortal may be swallowed up by life. Now the one who has fashioned us for this very purpose is God, who has

given us the Spirit as a deposit, guaranteeing what
is to come.

—2 CORINTHIANS 5:1–5

Paul continues:

I…would prefer to be away from the body and
at home with the Lord. So we make it our goal to
please him, whether we are at home in the body
or away from it. For we must all appear before the
judgment seat of Christ, so that each of us may
receive what is due us for the things done while in
the body, whether good or bad.

—2 CORINTHIANS 5:8–10

This passage has been subject to various interpretations.
First there are two interpretations on the eternal tent in
heaven. Some have thought this was a temporary body
since Paul indicates that it is received at death while the
resurrection body is received at the second coming of the
Messiah. However, Paul does not refer to it as a temporary
tent but as an eternal house. We really don't know what
Paul thought concerning what theologians have called
the "intermediate state." Is it some kind of conscious life
without a body, or is it a semiconscious life in awaiting the
resurrection? We simply are not told. Is there some kind
of temporary body? We do not know. Paul simply may not
be concerned about these details; and in referring to the
eternal house, he may simply be pointing to the ultimate
hope in the resurrection. He may indicate an intermediate
state when he says he would prefer to be away from the
body and to be at home with the Lord (v. 8). He does not
mention being in a body when he is with the Lord.

There are two primary interpretations of the judgment

seat of Messiah. The first is that this refers to the ultimate final judgment as also described in Revelation 20. The believers receive their rewards and suffer the loss of what was not built right in this life (the wood, hay, and straw mentioned in 1 Corinthians 3:12). However, the unbelievers are assigned to judgment.

The other interpretation is that this judgment is only the believers' judgment and is about rewards. It happens at the Second Coming and is to be distinguished from the other judgment at the end of the millennial age. Those who hold this position usually think that the judgment in Revelation 20 is only for those who will be condemned. However, the passage does not say this; it says that those who were not written in the Book of Life are cast into the lake of fire (v. 15). The implication is that some at this judgment did have their names written in the Book of Life.

GALATIANS

Paul's words concerning those who preach another gospel indicates that there is such a thing as being "eternally condemned." He does not explain the nature of that state but asserts that it is a real possibility:

> But even if we or an angel from heaven should preach a gospel other than the one we preached to you, let them be under God's curse! As we have already said, so now I say again: If anybody is preaching to you a gospel other than what you accepted, let them be under God's curse.
>
> —GALATIANS 1:8–9

Parallel to the passage in 1 Corinthians 6:9–10, Paul states in Galatians 5:19–21:

> The acts of the flesh are obvious: sexual immorality, impurity and debauchery; idolatry and witchcraft; hatred, discord, jealousy, fits of rage, selfish ambition, dissensions, factions and envy; drunkenness, orgies, and the like. I warn you, as I did before, that those who live like this will not inherit the kingdom of God.

Contrary to universalist beliefs, Paul does not qualify this exclusion. The language is most naturally read to imply a permanent exclusion.

EPHESIANS

As we noted in 2 Corinthians 1:22, Paul teaches that the presence of the Holy Spirit is a seal, a deposit or guarantee of our future everlasting life.

> And you also were included in Christ when you heard the message of truth, the gospel of your salvation. When you believed, you were marked in him with a seal, the promised Holy Spirit, who is a deposit guaranteeing our inheritance until the redemption of those who are God's possession—to the praise of his glory.
>
> —EPHESIANS 1:13–14

Through the gospel the Gentiles are now "heirs together with Israel, members together of one body, and sharers together in the promise in Christ Jesus" (3:6).

The context of this promise is again that wonderful eternal destiny for the believer that is part of the final end of creation.

Philippians

In Philippians 1 the imprisoned Paul affirms his confident hope that he will be faithful whether or not he will live or die. He states, "For to me, to live is Christ and to die is gain" (Phil. 1:21).

He states that to continue living in the body it will mean fruitful labor (v. 22). Yet he is torn for if he departs (in death and hence leaves his body) he will be with Messiah, which is better by far for himself (v. 23). Yet he is convinced that it is to their benefit that he remains (v. 24). Paul does not describe the state of being with Messiah. It does seem clear that no ceasing of conscious being with a later reconstitution in resurrection (as in Adventism) is contemplated.

In Philippians 3 Paul professes to desire to know the Messiah and the power of His resurrection, but also the fellowship of His sufferings (v. 10). Paul is already participating in His death and resurrection. The goal is "somehow, to attain to the resurrection from the dead" (v. 11). Paul continues to say that he has not yet obtained perfection, but he presses on to become all that he can be in the Messiah, to take hold of that for which Yeshua took hold of him. He presses on to win the prize for which God has called him heavenward (vv. 13–14). This again affirms the teaching of Paul that there is a significant reward for those who embrace faithfully fulfilling their calling.

That destiny in the age to come is again described as including a glorified body in terms similar to 1 Corinthians 15. In Philippians 3:20–21 we read:

> Our citizenship is in heaven. And we eagerly await a Savior from there, the Lord Jesus Christ, who, by the power that enables him to bring everything

under his control, will transform our lowly bodies
so that they will be like his glorious body.

COLOSSIANS

The idea of a glorious afterlife for true disciples of Yeshua
permeates the Epistles of Paul and also the whole New
Testament. The New Covenant Scriptures do not otherwise
make sense. So when we choose more explicit statements,
the reader should be aware that these statements are only
bringing out what is always in the background of the
meaning of the New Testament. So in Colossians 3:1-4 we
read:

> Since, then, you have been raised with Christ, set
> your hearts on things above, where Christ is seated
> at the right hand of God. Set your minds on things
> above, not on earthly things. For you died, and your
> life is now hidden with Christ in God. When Christ,
> who is your life, appears, then you also will appear
> with him in glory.

This text looks toward the Second Coming when all
true Yeshua-believers will receive glorified bodies and
enter into the glory of the age to come.

1 AND 2 THESSALONIANS

The Thessalonian correspondence includes very important
texts on the afterlife but mostly affirms the glorious
afterlife for followers of Yeshua.

First Thessalonians 2:19 asks us about one part of the
reward in the age to come: "What is our hope, our joy,
or the crown in which we will glory in the presence of
our Lord Jesus when he comes? Is it not you? Indeed, you

are our glory and joy." The rewards in the age to come are connected to relationships and responsibilities that are fitting to one's calling and attainment on earth. This is an important passage that shows that the hope of rewards is not a carnal type of reward.

Then in 1 Thessalonians 4:13–18 we read one of the most important passages in Scripture concerning the destiny of those who will reign with the Messiah. It is parallel to 1 Corinthians 15:

> Brothers and sisters, we do not want you to be uninformed about those who sleep in death, so that you do not grieve like the rest of mankind, who have no hope. For we believe that Jesus died and rose again, and so we believe that God will bring with Jesus those who have fallen asleep in him. According to the Lord's word, we tell you that we who are still alive, who are left until the coming of the Lord, will certainly not precede those who have fallen asleep. For the Lord himself will come down from heaven, with a loud command, with the voice of the archangel and with the trumpet call of God, and the dead in Christ will rise first. After that, we who are still alive and are left will be caught up together with them in the clouds to meet the Lord in the air. And so we will be with the Lord forever. Therefore encourage one another with these words.

This text again affirms the bodily destiny of those who are in the Messiah in the next life. Those who have died will be joined to those who are alive and all will be in their glorified bodies. They will meet the Lord in the air and will be with Him forever. The text does not say where we will go after we meet the Lord in the air, but other texts indicate that we return to earth with Him.

Second Thessalonians 1:5–10 presents a very important passage on being worthy to enter the Kingdom of God, in its future sense, and God's judgment on those who do not know God and do not obey the gospel.

> All this is evidence that God's judgment is right, and as a result you will be counted worthy of the kingdom of God, for which you are suffering. God is just: He will pay back trouble to those who trouble you and give relief to you who are troubled, and to us as well. This will happen when the Lord Jesus is revealed from heaven in blazing fire with his powerful angels. He will punish those who do not know God and do not obey the gospel of our Lord Jesus. They will be punished with everlasting destruction and shut out from the presence of the Lord and from the glory of his might on the day he comes to be glorified in his holy people and to be marveled at among all those who have believed.

The text provides two categories of exclusion from the future Kingdom of God: those who do not know God and those who do not obey the gospel of the Lord Yeshua. Now are these two categories only different ways of saying the same thing so that only those who have heard and obeyed the gospel will be saved? Or, is knowing God in some sense a broader category? We saw that Romans 1 and 2 give some indication that the category of knowing God is broader than those who have obeyed the gospel, but that rejecting the gospel places people in great danger. Two aspects of punishment are stated. The first is that the judged will be shut out; that is, excluded from His presence. However, the term used here for their final destiny is "everlasting destruction" (v. 9). This term is used by some interpreters to show that any experience of conscious suffering must be temporary and that ultimate destruction is the final end of the wicked.

Chapter 2 adds more information concerning the Second Coming and our gathering unto Him at that time, as described in 1 Thessalonians 4:16ff. This gathering will take place after the man of sin is revealed, also described as the Antichrist in historic theology. Those who follow him and his lies are said to be perishing: "They perish because they refuse to love the truth and so be saved" (2 Thess. 2:10).

However, the destiny of the saved is to share in the glory of the Lord Yeshua (v. 14).

THE LETTERS TO TIMOTHY

First Timothy 2:4–5 states that God "wants all men to be saved and to come to a knowledge of the truth. For there is one God and one mediator between God and man, the man Christ Jesus.

This passage is used by universalists; but again, it seems that they seek to make this passage say more than it is asserting. The view of the universalists is that if God desires all men to be saved, then how can the desire of God be thwarted? Of course the answer is that, though God has this desire, He has a greater desire that human beings be free; and this freedom comes with ability to resist God's desire and to be lost.

This letter, as all of Paul's letters, only makes sense in the context of his understanding of everlasting resurrection life. In 1 Timothy 4:8 we read that "godliness has value for all things, holding promise both for the present life and the life to come."

Verse 10 is a bit strange, for Paul says, "We have put our hope in the living God, who is the Savior of all men, and especially of those who believe." Is Paul saying that there is hope for those who have not explicitly believed in Him or merely that He is the Savior of all but especially to those who believe since unless His salvation is appropriated, it is of no effect?

In 2 Timothy 1:10 we read that the Messiah Yeshua "has destroyed death and has brought life and immortality to light through the gospel."

The hope of the elect in 2 Timothy 2:10 is that "they too may obtain the salvation that is in Christ Jesus, with eternal glory." Paul then quotes a poem or a confession hymn, a trustworthy saying:

> If we died with him, we will also live with him; if we endure, we will also reign with him. If we disown him, he will also disown us; if we are faithless, he will remain faithful, for he cannot disown himself.
> —2 TIMOTHY 2:11–13

We see the great hope of everlasting resurrection life for those who are in Him and the promise of reigning with Him if we endure in this life. We also note warning that we can disown Him and this will lead to a terrible consequence of being disowned, which looks like being lost. Though a human being may be faithless, God and Yeshua are always faithful (to their promise). Yeshua cannot be other than who He is, or He cannot disown Himself.

TITUS

Titus begins with the ringing hope of everlasting life where he describes the faith as

> the hope of eternal life, which God, who does not lie, promised before the beginning of time, and which now at his appointed season he has brought to light through the preaching entrusted to me by the command of God our Savior.
>
> —TITUS 1:2–3

Everlasting life is central to the gospel, and any secularized gospel that does not embrace the message of everlasting life is a false gospel.

In Titus 3:7 we read, "Having been justified by his grace, we might become heirs having the hope of eternal life."

EBEN ALEXANDER, MD

This neurosurgeon describes his near-death experience of heaven. He also, in a part of the book that won't be quoted here, meets relatives and an angel figure whom he later finds is a sister who was lost in infancy who had information that no one could have humanly known.

> Brilliant, vibrant, ecstatic, stunning....I could heap on one adjective after another to describe what this world looked and felt like, but they'd all fall short. I felt like I was being born. Not reborn, or born again. Just...born. Below me there was countryside. It was green, lush, and earthlike. It *was* earth...but at the same time it wasn't. It was like when your parents take you back to a place where you spent some years as a very young child. You don't know the place. Or at least you think you don't. But as you look

around, something pulls at you, and you realize that a part of yourself—a part way, deep down—does remember the place after all, and is rejoicing at being back there again. I was flying, passing over trees and fields, streams and waterfalls, and here and there, people. There were children, too, laughing and playing. The people sang and danced around in circles, and sometimes I'd see a dog, running and jumping among them, as full of joy as the people were. They wore simple yet beautiful clothes, and it seemed to me that the colors of those clothes had the same kind of living warmth as the trees and the flowers that bloomed and blossomed in the countryside around them. A beautiful, incredible dream world...except it wasn't a dream.[3]

CHRISTOPHER PAUL CARTER

Christopher Paul Carter claims that he is able to take mental journeys to heaven and that others can do so. His accounts are interesting. Are they visions? Sanctified imaginations?

There are lots of throne rooms (in heaven) to talk about. Every one of them has a specific atmosphere and purpose and it could easily take a lifetime to discover all of them. On one visit, the Lord handed me a golden book called the Courts of Heaven. It looked hundreds of pages thick and read like an encyclopedia. On every page was a picture of a specific room and a paragraph or two describing its attributes....The "Kingdom Palace" (Throne room) is so big it could hold city blocks....To describe this place adequately, I need words that I'm not sure exist in the English language. It is just too big and too grand to provide a worthy description, but I'll give it a try. Imagine a huge, rectangular room with columns supporting either side of a high, vaulted ceiling. The columns themselves were imposing because of their size, and the whole room looked to be made of glowing gold. Nothing was left untouched by the hand of a master craftsman. Everywhere I looked I would see ornate carvings and reliefs in various colors. Lining either side of the main walkway that led to the throne were huge, marble sculptures of angels and people, all depicting different parts of the story of God and His creation. The walkway that led to the throne was like rich, red carpet and the throne itself was set atop a flight of wide stairs. Sometimes angels were standing on either side of the Lord as He held court and at other times, the Lord would be milling about the grand room and talking with whosoever was there.[4]

He visits a cathedral-like building and describes this:

Then I noticed that at the very front of the room were massive, gold organ pipes, and there were layers of them stacked in ascending and descending order. I looked at the angel sitting on my right and said, "What is this place and what are we doing here?" Suddenly the organ lets out an enormous blast of sound and a heavenly choir, which I had not previously seen sitting to the right and left of the organ pipes, erupted with those famous lines from Handel's "Messiah": "King of kings! Forever and ever! And Lord of lords! Hallelujah! Hallelujah!" The sheer volume was enough to scare me silly and the angel, now laughing slightly, looked at me and said, "Choir practice."[5]

Chapter 9

HEBREWS, THE GENERAL EPISTLES, AND REVELATION

THE BOOK OF HEBREWS

The Book of Hebrews is written to Messianic Jews. Its authorship is uncertain, but its theology is consistent with Pauline theology, though with different emphases and language style. Hebrews speaks about the great salvation that has now been announced and confirmed with signs and wonders. This salvation is described as including Yeshua "bringing many sons to glory" (2:10). By His death He is said to "destroy him who holds the power of death—that is, the devil—and free those who all their lives were held in slavery by their fear of death" (vv. 14–15).

Yeshua is the mediator of a new covenant "that those who are called might receive the promised eternal inheritance" (9:15). The writer also tells us that a judgment is coming at the return of the Messiah, but His coming will bring salvation for those waiting for Him:

> Just as people are destined to die once, and after that to face judgment, so Christ was sacrificed once to take away the sins of many; and he will appear a second time, not to bear sin, but to bring salvation to those who are waiting for him.
>
> —HEBREWS 9:27–28

For those who "deliberately keep on sinning after" receiving "the knowledge of the truth, no sacrifice for sins is left, but only a fearful expectation of judgment and of raging fire that will consume the enemies of God" (10:26–27). Then in verse 31 we read, "It is a dreadful thing to fall into the hands of the living God." Also in verse 36 we are exhorted to persevere with these words: "You need to persevere so that when you have done the will of God, you will receive what he has promised." The text then quotes Habakkuk 2:3–4 and notes that the one who shrinks back will not please God. Of his readers he states, "We are not of those who shrink back and are destroyed, but of those who believe and are saved" (Heb. 10:39).

Hebrews warns of a severe and fearful judgment for those who deliberately continue in sin. The fire is said to consume, which would seem to support the idea of the eventual annihilation of the lost. Yet it must be more than just ceasing to be at death since *something terrible will be experienced.*

In Hebrews 12 the people of great faith are said to be a cloud of witnesses that surround us (v. 1). This indicates that they continue in existence and are somewhat aware of us. Our faith ultimately is about receiving a "kingdom that cannot be shaken" (v. 28). So while we worship and give thanks to God, we also are to maintain reverence and awe, "for God is a consuming fire" (v. 29).

The General Epistles

1 and 2 Peter

First Peter 1:4–5 speaks of the living hope we have, based on the resurrection of Yeshua from the dead. This hope is an inheritance that "can never perish, spoil or fade—kept in heaven for you, who through faith are shielded by God's power until the coming of the salvation that is ready to be revealed in the last time." The goal of our faith is the "salvation of our souls" (v. 9). The same hope of everlasting life in resurrection bodies that was emphasized by Paul is found in Peter's letters.

Peter promises those who are elders/shepherds of the flock that if they are faithful to their calling, "When the Chief Shepherd appears, you will receive the crown of glory that will never fade away" (5:4). What is this crown of glory? As Paul noted, it was at least in the joy of those who were presented to God for His glory and will be forever part of our joy.

Peter, in 2 Peter 2:9, promises that the godly will be ultimately rescued but that the unrighteous will be held "for the day of judgment, while continuing their punishment." This ultimate judgment is more than just staying dead. This seems to be consistent in New Testament pictures of judgment.

God's heart is that all would come to repentance and not perish (3:9). Perishing here is to be excluded from that good end of everlasting life with Yeshua. That God is holding back the judgment and giving time for people to repent does show that people will perish. Again, perishing can be taken as ceasing to be but could also be used metaphorically for continued existence but exclusion from fellowship with God.

1 John

First John 2:25 states that the Father "promised us, even eternal life." What will we be like when He comes? John tells us that when He appears, "we shall be like him, for we shall see him as he is" (3:2). First John 5:11–13 states:

> And this is the testimony: God has given us eternal life, and this life is in his Son. He who has the Son has life: he who does not have the Son of God does

not have life. I write these things to you who believe
in the name of the Son of God so that you may
know that you have eternal life.

In the language of John, as most scholars note, eternal
life begins in the present but continues into the age to
come and lasts forever.

Jude

Jude as well affirms the ultimate judgment of the
wicked in verses 14–16, where the non-canonical Book of
Enoch is quoted and states that when the Lord comes with
thousands of His saints, He will judge everyone and will
convict the ungodly of all the evil they have done. But we
are to wait for the mercy of the Lord who will bring us to
eternal life (v. 21).

Jude concludes with these words of encouragement in
verses 24 and 25:

> To him who is able to keep you from stumbling
> and to present you before his glorious presence
> without fault and with great joy— to the only God
> our Savior be glory, majesty, power and authority,
> through Jesus Christ our Lord, before all ages, now
> and forevermore!

The general Epistles end on a ringing affirmation of our
life in the age to come when Yeshua presents us before His
own presence and we enter into the glory of that age.

THE BOOK OF REVELATION

Revelation 2

The letters to the seven congregations in Revelation 2
already note that there is a future life after death and a

right to eat from the tree of life. This is given to the ones who overcome or are victorious (v. 7). This tree is pictured in Revelation 22 as a source of sustenance in the age to come. The second death is noted in Revelation 2:11 in the letter to Smyrna: the one who overcomes will not be hurt by the second death. In verse 26 in the letter to Thyatira, those who overcome are promised to exercise authority over the nations.

Revelation 3

In chapter 3, verses 4 through 6, those in Sardis who have been faithful are promised that they will be dressed in white, a symbol of purity, and their names will never be blotted out of the Book of Life (recorded in chapter 20, verse 15, as the book that records those who have everlasting life with Yeshua in the age to come). The Philadelphian congregation is told that Yeshua is coming soon (v. 11). He that overcomes will be made a pillar in the temple of God (v. 12). The name of God will be written on him, and the name of the New Jerusalem (v. 13). The Laodiceans are given the promise that overcomers will sit with Yeshua on His throne just as He sat down with the Father after He overcame (v. 21). This is a symbol of a position of authority.

All these letters point to a great reward for the faithful in the age to come. They emphasize a position of authority, purity, everlasting life, and joy.

Revelation 6

The opening of the fifth seal presents a picture of the souls who were slain because of the Word of God and their testimony; they are described as under the heavenly altar (v. 9). They cry out asking how long it will be until their blood is avenged (v. 10). They were given white robes and told it will be a little longer and until the full number of their fellow servants and brothers who were to be slain are killed (v. 11).

This sum total of martyrs completes a condition for the release of God's purposes on earth. The slain are visible but not yet resurrected. At least we can wonder how to fit this into the picture of life after death. This is a symbolic passage so we should not read too much into it, but it does provide some indication of an intermediate state before the resurrection.

Revelation 7

In Revelation 7:9 a great multitude from all nations, dressed in white, serve God day and night in His temple. Is this the position of the saints symbolically during the Tribulation or is this a picture of those who have died and are in the heavenly temple serving God? We cannot be too dogmatic. My view is that is symbolic of the saints on earth during the Tribulation.

Revelation 14

Revelation 14:14–20 describes two harvests of the earth. Many interpreters historically took the first to be the gathering of the believers to Yeshua. Verse 16 tells of the one who harvests the earth; in this interpretation He is Yeshua.

> So he who was seated on the cloud swung his sickle over the earth, and the earth was harvested.

Revelation 19

Revelation 19 presents the powerful vision of the return of Yeshua. His triumph and rule are described. We read in verses 7 and 8:

> The wedding of the Lamb has come, and his bride
> has made herself ready. Fine linen, bright and clean,
> was given to her to wear. (Fine linen stands for the
> righteous acts of God's people.)

The bride here is a corporate person, who is best and historically interpreted as the new covenant people of Yeshua. However, there are others who are not said to be the bride but are invited to the wedding. Who are they? Are they the nations that come into the Kingdom but are not included in the bride since they did not come to the Lord before the final events of His coming? Of course these are plausible ideas but not certain because we do not know how far to press symbolic and metaphorical language. In Revelation 21 the bride is the city, but here it is the people. Both are probably one. The city is where the people dwell. The bride would be in translated/resurrected form. The symbols and metaphors of this text teach that there is a wonderful afterlife for the redeemed.

The second harvest is the harvest of the clusters of grapes that are gathered into the winepress of God's wrath (v. 15). The judgment that takes place in the return of the Messiah is described in verses 17 through 21.

Revelation 20

We read that the beast (the Antichrist) and the false prophet were thrown into the lake of fire. In chapter 20, verses 1 through 3, an angel from heaven seized the dragon, the devil, or Satan, and bound him for 1,000 years. During this time, he cannot deceive the nations.

The next part of the vision in verses 4 through 6 shows those who were beheaded in martyrdom. They are alive again. They reigned with Messiah for 1,000 years. It is difficult to know how to harmonize this with Paul's earlier statements about the Second Coming when all who died in the Messiah are raised to new life and those alive at His coming are fully transformed and join them. Perhaps the text is not excluding others but only comforting the readers in their concern for the martyrs who in some cases were beheaded. We cannot think that only martyrs that were beheaded are alive again! This is called the first resurrection. Those who are part of it are not subject to what the text calls the second death. This is significant confirmation of the good destiny of those who die for their faith.

In verses 7 through 9 we read that Satan is loosed for a brief season and fosters one more rebellion. Fire from heaven devoured those who rebelled and followed Satan. The devil who deceived them is "thrown into the lake of burning sulfur, where the beast and the false prophet had been thrown. They will be tormented day and night forever and ever" (v. 10).

Here we read of three figures, two human and one non-human: the beast, the false prophet, and the devil. They are said to be tormented forever and ever, not just cease to be.

This is followed by one of the most foundational passages in the Bible on the last judgment and the destiny of human beings in the afterlife. Daniel 12:2–3 provides a context and background for this text.

> Then I saw a great white throne and him who was seated on it. The earth and the heavens fled from his presence, and there was no place for them. And I saw the dead, great and small, standing before the throne, and books were opened. Another book was opened, which is the book of life. The dead were

judged according to what they had done as recorded in the books. The sea gave up the dead that were in it, and death and Hades gave up the dead that were in them, and each person was judged according to what they had done. Then death and Hades were thrown into the lake of fire. The lake of fire is the second death. Anyone whose name was not found written in the book of life was thrown into the lake of fire.

—REVELATION 20:11–15

The question is, are the people thrown into the lake of fire destroyed totally or do they continue in conscious suffering as was said in verse 10 of the devil, the beast, and the false prophet? Who is in the Book of Life? We are certain that it includes all who embraced Yeshua; but were they not already resurrected before this? Or does it include all who embraced Yeshua who lived during the 1,000 year Millennium. Were there others included in the Book of Life who did not consciously embrace Yeshua in life but who responded rightly to God's revelation in nature, cultures, and conscience as some see as taught in Romans 2? We simply are not told.

I do believe that one thing is quite certain. Those who have taught that all the people who face this judgment are lost were certainly wrong. The text obviously is opening up the Book of Life because some of those at this judgment are found written in the Book of Life. Of course, exactly how this judgment is carried out is not presented, but the judgment is presented in a metaphorical vision with judgment books and a judge who would judge one person at a time. It will be much more supernatural than can be represented by a literal court scene.

Revelation 21

From this point on, Revelation 21 and 22 present a very powerful picture of life in the age to come. The reader of this book should just read these texts. Here are a few of the features: God will dwell in the midst of His people; He will wipe away all tears from all eyes; death, mourning, crying, and pain are no more; all is made new (21:3–5).

A new city is described in verses 10 through 21 as either a cube that is multistoried or a pyramid. One cannot be sure from the three dimensions of length and width of the base, which is a square of 1,400 miles or 2,200 kilometers. The height is also the same. How symbolic is the picture? The city is the bride, but the people who dwell there are the bride as well if we credit Revelation 19:7–8. The city and the new world are the inheritance of the overcomers. But the exclusionary verses are also strong.

> But the cowardly, the unbelieving, the vile, the murderers, the sexually immoral, those who practice magic arts, the idolaters and all liars—they will be consigned to the fiery lake of burning sulfur. This is the second death.
>
> —REVELATION 21:8

The picture again returns to the New Jerusalem called the bride of the Lamb, the Holy City. The glory of the foundations and the gates are described. The city shines as a precious jewel, like jasper. The city was pure gold and every kind of jewel decorated the foundations. The gates were pearl (vv. 18–21). There was no temple, for the presence of God Almighty and the Lamb is such that the whole is a temple reality (v. 22).

Beyond the city is a world with nations that continue as nations. The kings of these nations bring their splendor into the city (v. 24). Again, only those whose names are written in the Lamb's Book of Life can enter it (v. 27).

Revelation 22

In Revelation 22:1-5 we read the picture of a river of life. It is as clear as crystal and flows from the throne of God and the Lamb. There is a tree of life on both sides of the river and the nations are healed by its fruit. We read that the servants of the Lamb will see His face and serve Him. The light of God will be so great that no sun or lamp will be needed. The servants of the Lamb will reign forever.

Again we read the affirmation of the coming judgment from the mouth of Yeshua: "I will give to everyone according to what he has done" (v. 12); and that those who wash their robes "have the right to the tree of life and may go through the gates of the city" (v. 14).

Another word of exclusion follows: "Outside are the dogs, those who practice magic arts, the sexually immoral, the murderers, the idolaters and everyone who loves and practices falsehood" (v. 15).This text indicates the continued existence of those who are excluded, not their extinction.

One last exclusion verse is presented at the end of this chapter: adding or subtracting from this book as an inspired revelation will lead to experiencing the plagues described in the Book of Revelation and to preclusion from eating from the tree of life and in the Holy City (v. 19).

TODD BURPO

Todd Burpo, an evangelical pastor in the Midwest, wrote a compelling book on his son Colton's experience of heaven. It includes supernatural information about Todd's family that his child could not know. It has been made into a very compelling movie as well. It has done quite well at the box office.

Colton had a vision of the throne of God:

> It was big, Dad,...really, really big, because God is the biggest one there is. And he really, really loves us, Dad.[1]

> The city does not need the sun or the moon to shine on it, for the glory of God gives it light, and the Lamb is its lamp.[2]

Of the gates of heaven, he said:

> "They were made of gold and there were pearls on them." The heavenly city itself was made of something shiny, "like gold or silver." The flowers and trees in heaven were "beautiful," and there were animals of every kind.[3]

CONCLUSIONS

FREQUENTLY PEOPLE TAKE positions on the issue of heaven, hell, and the afterlife that do not comprehensively survey the texts that are relevant to the issue. Sometimes they do so because they follow confessions of faith that have taken such positions. Others do so because they want to find a conclusion and make one or a few texts normative and all other texts are deemphasized. Of course, it is in their interpretation of these few texts that filters everything. Texts that do not easily fit in are squeezed into a meaning so they will be made to fit or they are simply ignored. There is also the motive to be true to a confession of faith that is part of one's denomination, congregation, or stream. Such statements on heaven and hell are quite simple and normally black and white. I here outline the most common of positions on heaven, hell, and the afterlife in the age to come:

1. The first is the position of classic fundamentalism from the beginning of the twentieth century. This was parallel to what was held in Catholic and orthodox Christian circles, though the grounds for salvation or damnation were different. This Protestant view asserted that only those who had explicitly embraced the gospel or received Yeshua

would have a positive afterlife in heaven or in the age to come. This would include a time in heaven until the resurrection, among some interpreters. All others would suffer conscious torment forever. This was considered their just judgment. There would be different levels of penalty for the damned and rewards for the saved. Variants of this view stated that one must submit to Yeshua as Lord to be saved while others believed in the classical dispensationalist's view that one can receive Yeshua for salvation but never commit one's life to Him. They can live a carnal Christian life and be saved.

2. The second position is that the category of those saved will be greater than just those who we know to have explicitly embraced Yeshua in this life. This would be a response to the universal aspect of Yeshua as the *Logos*. Those who believe that this is a limited number (like John Wesley) and those who believe it is a larger but undetermined number argue from Romans 1 and 2 and John 1:9. Some argue that those in this category will embrace Yeshua in some way before they die or at least in the dying experience, though it may not be known to outside observers.

3. Most classical fundamentalists and Catholics before Vatican II believed that the lost will

suffer judgment and torment forever, though there will be different degrees of torment.

4. Some believe that the penalty for the lost is that they will just be destroyed or cease to be. When they die, that is it! It is their end.

5. Some believe that the penalty for the lost will be to suffer for a time according to their deserts but then they will cease to be.

6. Some believe in universal salvation, and that eventually all will be saved. Hell is often interpreted by these folks as purgatorial and temporary. The statements on its eternal aspect have to do with the quality of the judgment and not its duration.

Those who believe in a high view of Scripture assert that all the texts of the Bible present only truth in that which is being asserted. If they hold to the different views noted, they will argue their view by crediting some texts above others and interpreting the other texts accordingly, fitting them into what they consider more primary. *My view is that we have to credit all the texts and not try to too easily squeeze them into harmony.* This may leave some unresolved mysteries. However, I do want to assert strongly that the whole of the biblical evidence is quite clear that the ultimate destiny of the saved or righteous is on a renewed or new earth, not in heaven. This is most brilliantly argued by N. T. Wright in his *Surprised by Hope*.[1]

I present here a brief summary of the development of the biblical material and the conclusions that follow therefrom. I will not repeat all the references that can be looked up in the earlier sections of this book.

The earliest sections of the Bible do not present us with any clear description of the afterlife. In my view, the Patriarchs and the early Israelites certainly had a positive sense of an afterlife for the righteous. Such views were widespread among the peoples of the ancient Middle East. Anthropologists and archaeologists document burial practices that indicate the hope of an afterlife. The patriarchal statements about the dead being gathered to their ancestors means more than just placing their bones together.

This hope of an afterlife develops into the idea of a resurrection where the righteous of former generations are raised from the dead to participate in the age to come. We find especially in the psalmists the idea that the righteous will receive an afterlife that will balance the scales of justice while the wicked will come to a sad end. The psalms sometimes seem to indicate that the wicked will experience a terrible judgment. This is sometimes spoken of as total destruction. The common ideas of all people continuing in an afterlife of a shadowy kind is superseded by the hope of the righteous having an afterlife of triumph. The wicked either are ultimately destroyed or stay in the shadowy existence and suffer the consequences of an evil life. Those who are included in a positive afterlife are those who are said to be righteous. Being righteous has to do with the total sum of a person's life, the heart orientation to goodness. However, the Bible always emphasizes that one is dependent on the grace and mercy of God to be accepted as righteous. The orientation of the heart is an emphasis of the psalms.

The Book of Daniel presents a stark idea of final judgment. The Book of Daniel had a large influence in the days of the writing of the New Covenant Scriptures. Daniel shows both the righteous and the wicked raised from the dead. Some arise to everlasting life (a joyful existence) and some to everlasting shame and contempt. This looks like continued conscious suffering for the wicked, but some interpret the everlasting shame as the ultimate memory of their judgment by others and not that the wicked continue to exist and suffer forever. This is a speculation not asserted in the text.

The New Covenant Scriptures emphasize the everlasting joyful resurrection life for the righteous and everlasting condemnation for the wicked. The righteous are those who are in Yeshua and have received His transforming grace. There are texts that speak of everlasting destruction and texts that speak of conscious suffering after the judgment. There are texts that seem to indicate an everlasting suffering in this judgment, especially Revelation 20. C. S. Lewis noted that the texts on the destruction of the wicked (ceasing to exist) and texts on continued punishment and suffering were both in the Bible.[2] This has prompted some to hold that there is continued conscious suffering for a time but then ultimate destruction. However, Lewis noted that the everlasting suffering texts need to be credited. He came up with a theory that the wicked are passing into greater and greater destruction and personality disintegration but never fully disappear without a trace. He knew that this was a speculative solution to the two types of text.[3] I do want to emphasize that contrary to some who used a very few texts in Paul to teach universal salvation for all, the overwhelming evidence of numerous texts teach a separation of the righteous and the wicked and the ultimate exclusion of the wicked from the Kingdom of God in its future everlasting manifestation.

Those who hold that the destiny of the wicked is to simply cease to exist at their death have to answer several problems. One is that many atheists are happy with the idea of just ceasing to exist at death. Some really do not want a continued life after death, as hard as that may be for some believers to understand. In addition, the Bible does say that there is a horrible judgment awaiting the wicked. Just ceasing to exist does not fit the biblical description of how horrible this judgment is.

So this brings me to some final conclusions:

1. The Bible teaches that a glorious future life after death awaits the righteous. It is a life on a new or renewed earth in resurrection bodies.

2. The new covenant emphasizes that this glorious afterlife is promised to all who are in Yeshua. Part of the gospel is to give people assurance of this afterlife in their embrace of the King and the gospel of the Kingdom. The Bible does not present salvation for those who merely believe but do not embrace Yeshua as Lord. It is God's grace that enables people to do so.

3. The new covenant assumes that the righteous from the pre-Yeshua period are included as those who are in Him and will have a part in this glorious future.

4. The wicked will have a terrible judgment of torment and suffering. Whether it lasts forever or is of limited duration but of different lengths and suffering for different people is hard to finally conclude from the texts. We are safe in just noting that it is more than the wicked ceasing to exist at death. A terrible afterlife awaits the wicked. This should be enough to produce legitimate fear in those who study the texts.

5. There are some grounds for hope that those who are included in the salvation of Yeshua is wider than just those who have consciously embraced the gospel. However, the Bible seems pessimistic about the response of those who only have God's revelation in nature and culture. While there is somewhat of a possibility (John 1:9 and Romans 1 and 2), we should orient ourselves to the need for all people to hear the gospel to assure them of a good everlasting destiny.

6. It is difficult to credit universalism as having a real basis in the Bible. This view is only held by embracing a few texts that are easily interpreted in other ways and ignoring that many numerous texts that speak of the destiny of the wicked and their exclusion from the future Kingdom of life.

NOTES

INTRODUCTION

1. Rob Bell, *Love Wins* (New York: HarperOne, 2011).

2. Douglas Campbell, *The Deliverance of God* (Grand Rapids, MI: Eerdmans, 2009).

3. David Edwards and John Stott, *Evangelical Essentials* (Downers Grove, IL: InterVarsity Press, 1988), accessed November 8, 2016, http://www.truthaccordingtoscripture.com/documents/death/judgement-hell.php#.WCZw-forLIU.

CHAPTER 1
THE AFTERLIFE IN THE TORAH

1. Douglas Neff, *Dante's Inferno in Modern English* (Cork: BookBaby, 2011).

CHAPTER 2
THE HISTORICAL/PROPHETIC BOOKS

1. H. A. Baker, *Visions of Heaven* (New Kensington, PA: Whitaker House, 1973), 53.

2. Ibid., 57–58.

3. Ibid, 70.

4. Ibid., 88–89.

5. Ibid., 89.

6. Ibid., 90.

CHAPTER 3
THE POETIC BOOKS AND THE AFTERLIFE

1. G. K. Chesterton, *The Everlasting Man* (New York: Todd, Mead, and Co., 1925).

2. Thomas Welch, "Oregon's Amazing Miracle" in *The Thomas Welch Story* (Dallas, TX: Christ for the Nations, 1976), accessed October 27, 2016, http://www.freecdtracts.com/testimony/thomas_welch.htm.

3. Kenneth Hagin, *I Believe in Visions* (Old Tappan, NJ: Revell, 1972), 5–6, accessed October 27, 2016, http://www.devotional.net/uploads/147/104578.pdf.

CHAPTER 4
THE PROPHETS

1. Raymond Moody, *Life After Life* (Atlanta, GA: Mockingbird Books, 1975), 55.

2. Maurice Rawlings, *Beyond Death's Door* (Nashville: Thomas Nelson, 1978), 19–20.

3. Ibid., 81–82.

4. Ibid., 82.

5. Ibid., 94–95.

6. Ibid., 97.

CHAPTER 5
THE SYNOPTIC GOSPELS AND THE AFTERLIFE

1. C. S. Lewis, *Mere Christianity* (New York: Macmillan, 1952).

2. N. T. Wright, *Surprised by Hope* (New York: HarperCollins, 2007).

3. Lewis, *Mere Christianity*.

4. Rebecca Springer, *Within Heaven's Gates* (New Kensington, PA: Whitaker House, 1984), 18–19.

5. Ibid., 22–23.

6. Ibid., 33–34.

7. Ibid., 84–85.

8. "Holy, Holy, Holy, Lord God Almighty" is a hymn written in 1826 by Bishop Reginald Heber and composed and arranged by John B. Dykes.

CHAPTER 6
THE GOSPEL OF JOHN

1. Wright, *Surprised by Hope*.

2. John Sanders, *No Other Name* (Grand Rapids, MI: Eerdmans, 1992), 249–251.

3. Rick Joyner, *The Final Quest* (Charlotte, NC: Morning Star, 1996).

CHAPTER 7
THE BOOK OF ACTS

1. Howard Strom, *My Descent into Death* (London: Clairview, 2000), 20–21.

CHAPTER 8
THE PAULINE EPISTLES

1. Sanders, *No Other Name*.

2. "Our Wesleyan Heritage," United Methodist Communications, accessed November 5, 2016, http://www.umc.org/what-we-believe/our-wesleyan-heritage.

3. Eben Alexander, *Proof of Heaven* (New York: Simon and Shuster, 2012), 38–39.

4. Christopher Paul Carter, *In the Palaces of Heaven* (Mt. Pleasant, NC: Dwelling Place Ministries, 2013), 54.

5. Ibid., 61.

CHAPTER 9
HEBREWS, THE GENERAL EPISTLES, AND REVELATION

1. Todd Burpo, *Heaven Is for Real: A Little Boy's Astonishing Trip to Heaven and Back* (Nashville, TN: Thomas Nelson, 2012), 100.

2. Ibid., 104.

3. Ibid., 105.

CONCLUSIONS

1. Wright, *Surprised by Hope.*

2. Lewis, *Mere Christianity.*

3. Ibid.

ABOUT THE AUTHOR

D R. DANIEL JUSTER received his BA from Wheaton College, his MDiv from McCormick Theological Seminary, did two years in the philosophy of religion program of Trinity Evangelical Divinity School, and received his ThD from New Covenant International Seminary. Dr. Juster has been involved in the Messianic Jewish movement since 1972. He was the founding president and general secretary of the Union of Messianic Jewish Congregations for nine years; the senior leader of Beth Messiah Congregation, Rockville, Maryland, for twenty-two years; and presently is a member of the apostolic team that governs Tikkun International Ministries. Tikkun International is an umbrella organization for an apostolic network of leaders, congregations, and ministries who share a common commitment—namely the restoration of Israel and the Church. Dr. Juster is also the director of the Tikkun America of congregations; and as such, he provides oversight to some twenty congregations in the United States. He presently ministers personally under the name of Restoration from Zion, a Tikkun ministry.

Tikkun is committed to (1) training; (2) sending out and supporting congregational planters in the United States, Israel, and other countries; (3) fostering Jewish ministry in local churches; (4) helping to support an international network of Bible and graduate schools for training leaders for the Jewish vineyard and for work in the rest of the Church (presently there are schools in Odessa, Moscow; Buenos Aires, Argentina; and Zimbabwe).

Dr. Juster has authored several books, including *Jewish Roots: A Foundation of Biblical Theology*; *Dynamics of Spiritual Deception*; *Jewishness and Jesus*; *The Biblical World View: An Apologetic*; *Relational Leadership*; *The Irrevocable Calling*; *One People, Many Tribes*; and *Mutual Blessing*. He has been a featured speaker at many conferences, both nationally and internationally.

Presently, Dan and his wife, Patty, spend most of their year in Israel near Jerusalem and four months' travel in the United States. He has three married children and nine grandchildren who live in Israel.

CONTACT THE AUTHOR

Email: danieljuster@gmail.com